STRIKE!

To Grace ~ Here's wishing you the courage of Mother Jones!

STRIKE!

Mother Jones

& the Colorado Coal Field War

Lois Ruby
11/2015

Lois Ruby

Filter Press, LLC
Palmer Lake, Colorado

Library of Congress Cataloging-in-Publication Data
Ruby, Lois.
Strike: Mother Jones and the Colorado Coal Field War / Lois Ruby.
p. cm.
Includes bibliographical references.
ISBN 978-0-86541-141-8 (pbk.: alk. paper)
ISBN 978-0-86541-125-8 (hardcover.: alk. paper)
1. Jones, Mother, 1837-1930–Juvenile literature. 2. Labor leaders–United States–Biography–Juvenile literature. 3. Women in the labor movement–United States–Biography–Juvenile literature. 4. Coal Strike, Colo., 1913-1914–Juvenile literature. 5. Coal miners–Labor unions–Organizing–Colorado–History–20th century–Juvenile literature I. Title.
HD8073.J6R83 2012
331.88092–dc23
[B]
2012021763

First edition 2012

Cover & Interior Design by Robert Schram
Bookends Publication Design
303-443-8277 / bookendsdesign@earthlink.net

Printed in the United States of America

Dedication

For the brave souls at Ludlow—
those who survived, and those who did not.
And for the children of Mary Harris "Mother" Jones,
who never lived to know the fearless
and uncompromising woman
their mother truly was.

Contents

Mary Harris "Mother" Jones, 1837–1930

PROLOGUE

Mount San Rafael Hospital Trinidad, Colorado

MOTHER JONES SAT ON HER BED, a blanket wrapped loosely around her shoulders. She grasped the ends of it in her gnarled hands. The room held a bracing cold that aggravated her arthritis, but she was used to this pain. She was under arrest at Mount San Rafael Hospital. Though she wasn't sick, this would be her jail for nine weeks. She was allowed no visitors save her lawyer, no newspapers or books, no mail. Her isolation was so complete that even the guards outside her room night and day were forbidden to talk to her.

It wasn't the first time she'd been arrested, nor would it be the last. In West Virginia two years earlier, she'd been tried and convicted of murder. For three months, she lived under the threat of death by firing squad, until the charges were suddenly dropped and she was freed. All through that ordeal, she'd been defiant, saying "I can raise as much hell in jail as anywhere," and indeed she did. But now she was in her late seventies, plagued by arthritis, and this incarceration troubled her more than the others had. Still, she would allow no one—not even the Sisters of Charity, who ran the hospital—to see her dejection as she hung her head in her aching hands.

A few miles away on that frigid morning of January 21, thousands of women protested her captivity on the streets of Trinidad. How it would have delighted Mother Jones, and how her sagging spirits would have soared, if only she'd known that their peaceful demonstration would come to be called the Mother Jones Riot.

CHAPTER ONE

The Mother Jones Riot Trinidad, Colorado: January 21, 1914

SARAH SLATOR WATCHED THE MEN of the Colorado National Guard sitting high and haughty on their horses in front of the post office. Seemed like there were a hundred of them, maybe more, tensed and ready for the throngs of women marching toward them.

Sarah had come the thirteen miles from Ludlow Tent Colony northwest of Trinidad to join the hundreds who'd been arriving all morning by train from various parts of Colorado. Imagine! All those wives, mothers, sisters, and daughters of striking coal miners marching shoulder-to-shoulder toward the soldiers. Though it was mid-week, they wore their Sunday finery and were bundled into their least threadbare coats and hats and gloves. An Italian immigrant woman led the parade, proudly carrying an American flag.

The crowd thundered across the bridge over a frozen river known as the Purgatoire. Everybody in the coal camps called it the Picketwire, fitting because miners had been on strike for four months, **picketing** night and day. They picketed the train depot in Ludlow and the entrance to the coal mines, trying to keep strikebreakers away. They'd been picketing faithfully ever since the men had gone out on strike in the fall. Winter had set in miserably early, with a blizzard on the day the strike began in September.

Today, though, wasn't about picketing, but it was indirectly about miners. Today's demonstration was to be a peaceful march to protest the arrest of Mary Harris "Mother" Jones, the much-admired, fierce defender of the rights of miners and laborers. She was being held prisoner at the Sisters of Charity hospital on the northern edge of Trinidad.

Sarah Slator watched, then joined the march. She was sixteen. Some coal miners' daughters her age were already wives and mothers. They carried babies in their arms or in slings tied around their shoulders or on their backs. Or they were slowed by toddlers grasping their coattails, scurrying to keep up. Sarah wasn't married and wasn't weighed down by a baby.

She marched with the others up Commercial Street and past the Columbian Hotel. Behind them trailed a small band of fathers and husbands and big brothers, protecting the women. Banners fluttered in the frigid air like sheets on a clothesline. One read, GOD BLESS MOTHER JONES. Another one read, MOTHER JONES HAS NOT DONE ANYTHING THAT WE WOULD NOT DO!

Sarah knew all about Mother Jones; everyone did. They knew she had spent her life traveling to mining camps and textile mills, loudly voicing her anger over poor working conditions and low wages. In Pennsylvania and West Virginia, Mother Jones led demonstrations and had been arrested with the protestors. In Colorado, they'd all heard her make her rabble-rousing fiery speeches about

joining a union to work together to get the mining companies to treat their workers fairly.

Someone in the crowd started singing—maybe it was that Welsh woman, Mary Hannah Thomas, who fancied herself an opera singer. All around Sarah, women's voices rose as strong as their confidence:

> The union forever, hurrah, boys, hurrah!
> Down with the militia, up with the law.
> For we're coming, Colorado, we're coming all the way,
> Shouting the battle cry of union![1]

Rounding the corner from Commercial Street to Main, the women at the head of the line gasped. A **phalanx** of cavalrymen blocked the path ahead. Shock rippled down the line of the parade. Mothers clasped their children's hands even tighter.

Brigadier General John Chase ordered his men to draw their sabers as Sarah and the other protesters approached. If the women kept their course and their courage, and the National Guardsmen didn't back down, they would soon be face to face.

The women of Trinidad and the Ludlow Tent Camp marched demanding the release of Mother Jones. When they faced the drawn sabers of the National Guard on horseback, they did not back down.

The "hurrah, boys, hurrah!" battle cry faded to a wavering murmur, but still the women advanced, and Sarah followed.

"Turn back!" General Chase shouted at the women.

The marchers slowed but kept on, straight toward the menacing line of men on horseback. What happened next depends on who tells the tale.

Sarah herself gave two versions of the story afterward. In the first, she said that something spooked Chase's horse, and when it reared, the startled general fell to the ground.

Later, she told it this way: From high on his horse, General Chase came near enough to kick her breast. But his boot was locked in the stirrup. He tried to loosen his foot and couldn't. The jerky effort caused his horse to stumble and bolt into another horse fixed to a buggy, and that's why he fell off his mount.

In the version by another eyewitness, Sarah Slator caught the general's eye, and he warned her, "Get back there!" She stood frozen, and Chase again warned her to retreat before that alleged vicious kick occurred.[2] The general had been so unkind to the protesters and spectators that when he finally loosened his boot trapped in the stirrup, they laughed at the ridiculous, ample-sized, pompous officer flailing on the ground.

How embarrassed and furious he must have been as he scrambled back onto his horse. He began swinging his revolver through the crowd, shouting to his men, "Ride down the women! Ride down the women!"

The soldiers eagerly complied. They spurred their horses onward, waving the flat sides of their sabers and their gun butts at the crowd.

Mrs. James Lanigan was the first knocked to the ground by a hit with the side of a saber. Defenseless against the militia, protesters hurled sticks and stones and bottles, as well as ugly names. Some screamed, and children wailed, as they all scattered to avoid being trampled under the horses' feet. It's easy to imagine the panic and terror these women and children felt facing angry soldiers with sabers raised. The violence escalated. A few women darted into doorways, shops, and yards, their genteel hats flying into the mud.

Others didn't escape so easily. Soldiers thrust their weapons toward the women's backs. A few fell to the ground, shielding babies still in their arms. Mrs. Thomas Braley tried to protect her face and suffered slashes to her hands. Mrs. Maggie Hammons suffered a slash across her forehead. Mrs. George Gibson's ear was nearly sliced off. Ten-year-old Robert Arguello was punched in the face. A cavalryman chased Mrs. Verna, yanked an American flag out of her hands, and allowed his horse to knock her to the ground where her coat soaked up icy mud. The smell of blood floated on the frozen air.

Mary Hannah Thomas hadn't intended to be in the thick of the action. She was actually on her way to the beauty parlor, not marching with the protesters, when she walked into the mounted soldiers. The soldiers later referred to her "saucy hostility" and accused her of sparking the rebellion. Maybe that was because she threw an umbrella at a soldier.[3]

Mary Thomas was a feisty woman, the daughter of one miner and bride of another and as brazen as her flaming red hair. She'd always loved the excitement of a bristling encounter, and so now she taunted the soldier: "You go on and go wash your dirty clothes you have on before you order me off the sidewalk."[4] He yanked at her coat; she scratched and clawed him. She was arrested.

And what of Sarah Slator? Five militiamen spun her around, one grinning as he smashed his rifle butt down on her right foot. She darted up Main Street as quickly as she could with a battered foot. In front of Zimmerman Book Store, she hid behind a telephone pole. A soldier jabbed his sword toward her, splintering the wooden pole.

"Break your sword, I don't care!" she shouted.

He swung twice more, but she was quick, and he missed.

Sarah heard another soldier threaten a woman pulling her three-year-old son along as she tried to escape the violent attacks. The soldier bellowed, "You'll get this bayonet if you don't hurry."

"You wouldn't dare," the mother said stubbornly.

"Oh, you think I am afraid?" taunted the soldier.

Sarah jumped into the fight: "I don't think you are afraid. You're so low you could do anything."[5]

For this, Sarah ended up in jail, along with Mary Thomas and her two children, plus five other women, all of them herded like livestock. As one soldier said, "When women sink beneath our respect, they need to be treated like cattle."[6]

Weeks passed before Sarah Slator, Mary Thomas, and the rest of the women and their children were released from jail.[7] But not without leaving behind some memories for their jailers. Mother Jones had trained women protesters to "sleep all day and sing all night" while imprisoned. "Say you're singing to the babies," she told them.[8]

Mary Thomas took Mother Jones at her word. She led the women in nonstop patriotic and union songs, sung as rollicking lullabies. They screeched and sang all through the night, unnerving the jail guards—especially when male prisoners on the other side of the small jail, and crowds swarming in the alley behind the jail, all joined in the singing. Meanwhile, Mary's children threw everything they could lift out a broken window and handily vandalized the jailhouse bathroom.[9] It was a merry adventure for them all.

Mother Jones got word of the riot in her hospital-prison a few miles away. She must have felt such smug satisfaction knowing that she'd inspired this motley army of rebellious women.

CHAPTER TWO

Fire Eater

MOTHER JONES HAD BEEN JAILED without criminal charges. Her captor was the same Brigadier General John Chase who confronted Sarah Slater during the Women's March. He was a Denver eye doctor and a part-time member of the Colorado National Guard. Mother Jones's "crime" was rabble-rousing—calling meetings, making speeches, and organizing demonstrations to aid laborers in their conflicts with the owners of southern Colorado coal mines.

Women of her era seldom made such public appearances, but there she was on every platform from stages to tree stumps, across the country, inciting people to lay down their tools, silence their machines, and go out on **strike**. The demonstrations she organized occasionally mushroomed into near-riots, not unlike the one in Trinidad that January day in 1914.

Despite the best intentions and sacrifices of the Trinidad protesters, Mother Jones continued to be held incommunicado. That meant she was not allowed to have contact with the outside world and was under twenty-four hour military guard. She was not released from the clutches of General Chase and the Sisters of Charity for eight more weeks. But during that time, her influence never waned.

In the years that Mother Jones led labor campaigns (between the 1870s and 1920s), workers and their families heard her electrifying words and took action, sometimes violently. Her labor campaigns reached streetcar operators in New York and San Francisco, female bottle washers in Wisconsin, copper miners in Arizona, and railroad workers in the Pacific Northwest. The children toiling fourteen hours a day in the textile mills of Pennsylvania and the coal mines of West Virginia were of special concern to her.

It was in Colorado, however, in 1913 and 1914 that she was most forceful and most controversial. To the men she called the "slaves of the caves," and to their wives and children, Mother Jones was an angel of mercy. To the militia, she was a bad-mouthed, heartless, troublesome creature and the "grandmother of agitators." To the owners and overseers of the coal industry, she was simply "the most dangerous woman in America."

If you study pictures of Mother Jones, you'll see that she looks different from one photograph to the next. In one, she's a kindly, wrinkled old soul; in the next, her narrowed eyes seem to pierce the viewer.

Journalists of her day described her as a sweet-faced old woman, short and stout. Her constant uniform was a black dress with a white lacy bodice. The gown fell to swollen ankles that poured over high-top shoes. She walked with a slight limp as she tramped along railroad tracks and dusty roads or over miles and miles of mountainous paths. Often she wore hip boots for slogging through muddy creeks and ravines. A flowered black bonnet shaded her eyes and sat

Although she looked like a sweet grandmother, Mother Jones was called the Most Dangerous Woman in America. She was also called the Miner's Angel and Labor's Hell Raiser.

lightly on her cloud of snowy curls. Steel-rimmed glasses that perched on her nose highlighted gunmetal-blue, sparkling eyes that were one moment playful and the next moment critical and blaming.

She appeared to be a gentle, loving grandmother whose lap often held children. But when she spoke, chandeliers in concert halls swayed. Her high **falsetto** voice with an Irish brogue bellowed, even over an audience of thousands.

"I am on the warpath here for the miners,"[1] Mother Jones shouted. "We will all go to glory together, or we will all die and go down together!"[2]

She was called a fire-eater when she stirred a crowd into a froth of excitement and determination. "She is at once as gentle as a cooing dove and as fierce as a lioness," one writer said about her public speaking style. Said another, she "had a vocabulary that caused many a mule skinner to hang his head in shame, and a voice that could out-shout a whole platform of bull-chested orators."[3]

The words that came from her sweet, pursed lips were seldom ladylike. In fact, she warned women, "Whatever the fight, don't be ladies!" Many called her vulgar and foul-mouthed, but as she herself said with a twinkle of humor, "That is the way we ignorant working people pray."[4]

Little is known about her early life. We know that Mary Harris was born in Ireland either in 1830, as she claimed, or in 1837, as most historians believe. She came to Toronto, Canada, with her family when she was a girl. She may have finished high school before she began teaching school. Then again, maybe not, since teachers back then simply had to read a chapter ahead of their students. Later in her life, she was asked if she ever went to college.

FAMOUS CONTEMPORARIES OF MOTHER JONES

Mary Harris "Mother" Jones lived from 1837 to 1930. Her life span overlapped with many important people, including—

Nelly Bly	1864–1922	Fearless female journalist
Al Capone	1899–1947	Notorious gangster
Samuel Clemens/ Mark Twain	1835–1910	One of America's greatest authors
Bessie Coleman	1892–1926	First female African American aviator
Thomas Edison	1847–1941	Inventor of the light bulb, among other things
Albert Einstein	1879–1955	Physicist who developed theory of relativity $E=MC^2$
Mohandes "Mahatma" Ghandi	1869–1948	Indian liberator, leading proponent of effective nonviolent protest
Scott Joplin	1867–1917	Musician noted for ragtime piano music
Florence Nightingale	1820–1910	Legendary war nurse
Herman "Babe" Ruth	1895–1948	New York Yankees right fielder and great hitter
Ida B. Wells	1862–1931	Daring African American civil rights warrior
Victoria Woodhull	1838–1927	Suffragist and candidate for U.S. president in 1872
Alice Paul	1885–1977	Suffragist who chained herself to the White House fence to draw attention to woman suffrage
Elizabeth Cady Stanton	1815–1902	Along with Susan B. Anthony, she was leader of the early woman suffrage movement in the U.S.

She replied, in her usual feisty manner, "I graduated from the college of hard knocks. That is my college—hunger, persecution and suffering—and I wouldn't exchange that college for all the university dudes on the face of God's earth."[5]

Mary's brief teaching career ended when she moved to Chicago to become a dressmaker. She said she preferred sewing to bossing children around. Chicago did not hold her for long, however. In those days, a woman needed to find a husband before she was condemned to spinsterhood. And so, she decided to move on.

CHAPTER THREE

Disaster Strikes 1860–1877

IN 1860, JUST AS THE CIVIL WAR WAS STARTING, Mary Harris packed up her few belongings and moved to Memphis, Tennessee. There, in the city along the Mississippi River, she met George Jones. He was an iron molder, and he told her how miserable it was to work and breathe in a shop with open flames, hissing steam, and very poor ventilation. He was active in a labor union, which supported the rights of workers to gain higher pay and safer working conditions. Soon Mary was convinced that labor unions were the answer to the problems of poor working people.

Mary and George married and eventually brought four babies into their home. But Memphis in the 1860s wasn't a pleasant place. Men who had traveled the world thought that Memphis was the "filthiest and most foul smelling city on earth."[1] Summer rains and thick humidity bred swarming mosquitoes, the kind that carried disease. It was not known until 1901 that mosquitoes were the source of the yellow fever epidemics that devastated Memphis not once, but six times in the 1800s. Victims of the disease fer flu-like symptoms, after which the lucky ones recovered. For others, especially during a massive epidemic, symptoms worsened into severe bleeding, black vomiting, seizures, coma, kidney and liver failure, brain dysfunction, and death.

Fierce rains drenched Memphis in the summer of 1867. Mosquitoes thrived, bringing a major outbreak of disease. By the end of the epidemic, 550 people had lost their lives to yellow fever. In a week's time, Mary Harris Jones's husband and all four children lay dead. Now, she was a childless widow in her thirties. Perhaps she wondered why only she survived and decided she was spared to do important work that would help others. Alone and grieving, she returned to Chicago.

There she took up dressmaking again, this time opening her own shop. But she did not like or respect the rich women she sewed for. "Parlor parasites" she called them, "ignorant geese" who wore five dollars' worth of makeup on their faces and bought toothbrushes for their dogs. Mary was far more comfortable with poor working women like herself.

The loss of her family was more than enough sorrow for one person, yet major tragedy struck in Chicago as well. In October 1871, a now-famous cow kicked over a lantern in Mrs. O'Leary's barn, and the hay began to burn, then the barn with it, then the fence around it. The fire leaped to other buildings, and Chicago became a cauldron of raging flames for three days. When the fire finally settled, one-sixth of the city, one hundred thousand buildings, had burned to the ground.

Mary beat her way through the stagnant smoke and stumbled around the ruins to find that the dressmaking shop had burned to the ground. Nothing was left for her in Chicago.

Few details of Mary's life between 1871 and the end of the century have survived. In her autobiography, she skips over whole chunks of her life and either lies or misremembers about others. We know that she was involved in The Great Upheaval, a fierce and bloody Pennsylvania railroad strike in 1877. We also know that twenty years later, she organized rallies in Pittsburgh to bolster the spirits of miners in a nationwide coal walkout that ended in success for the strikers.

Perhaps to triumph over the tragedies that she had experienced, she boldly reinvented herself in a strong, unmistakable persona, proclaiming her new identity as Mother Jones, defender of downtrodden workers everywhere.

Mother Jones left Chicago after the fire of 1871 destroyed the center of the city and left 100,000 people homeless.

erhood was at the center of the family circle,"
liott Gorn muses, "Mother Jones widened
embrace the entire family of labor."[2]

So, in her widow clothes and sturdy high-top shoes, she began to crisscross America as a labor organizer. "I live in the United States, but I do not know exactly in what place," Mother Jones once said. "My address is like my shoes; it travels with me wherever I go."[3]

And she kept on going! Huge crowds gathered to hear her fiery speeches urging people to join trade unions, stand up for their rights, and strike when all reasonable negotiations failed. Only through collective bargaining, the strength of numbers, would they bring about changes in their working conditions.

Would fifteen thousand be a large enough number to make a difference? Picture Mother Jones organizing such a parade of striking miners through the streets of Wilkes-Barre, Pennsylvania, in October 1900. Later in the week, she led one thousand miners and fifty women in wagons into the coal center near Wilkes-Barre, determined to stop strikebreakers from entering the caves to dig coal. Not only did this contingent of banner-waving, angry strikers stop traffic in town for two hours, but the mine operators gave up and closed down the mines for the day.[4] Mother Jones relished this kind of high jinks!

Or picture her in this scene, which she loved to tell to anyone who'd lend an ear. This would have been in West Virginia around 1903. She was in a one-horse rig, leading a column of striking miners toward a non-unionized coal camp. They were stopped by mine guards with machine guns. She looked over the scene and calmly slid down off the rig. She sauntered up to one of the machine guns, patted its muzzle, and said to the gunman behind it,

"Listen, you. Fire one shot today and 800 men in those hills will not leave one of your gang alive." The gunmen hastily let her and the others pass. Later, when Mother Jones was asked about those 800 miners in the hills, she said that, if there were miners in the hills, she didn't know a thing about it. "I realized we were up against it, and something had to be done," she said, "so I pulled the dramatic stuff on them thugs."[5]

Through her boundless determination and flair for drama, Mother Jones inspired laborers who looked to her for leadership in their struggles. Calling these workers "my boys and girls," she promised to live and work among

Mother Jones with President and Mrs. Calvin Coolidge and Theodore Roosevelt Jr. She met with several presidents to seek better working conditions for miners and for enforceable child labor laws.

them and to lead them fearlessly through tough times, even past machine guns. She also promised to take their pleas to U.S. presidents, and she did. She personally spoke to five presidents between 1897 and 1929: William McKinley, Theodore Roosevelt, William H. Taft, Woodrow Wilson, and Calvin Coolidge.

She told workers, especially the striking Colorado coal miners, that they could achieve safer working conditions and higher wages. She channeled her own energy and courage into them to wage the fights that loomed ahead. She gave them what money, food, and other necessities she could raise from audiences and from the United Mine Workers union. She assured miners that if they and their families would make the bitter sacrifices, they would eventually taste the sweet fruits of justice.

However, she could not promise them victory.

CHAPTER FOUR

Tumbling Down a Chute

"I AM BEING HELD A PRISONER INCOMMUNICADO in a damp underground cell," the cantankerous Mother Jones wrote in March 1914.[1] She was moved to a cell in the basement of the Huerfano County Courthouse, in Walsenburg, Colorado. Even though the jail had been condemned as unfit for human habitation, she spent five weeks there, the dampness seeping into her old bones. "It was cold, it was a horrible place. I had sewer rats . . . to fight, and all I had was a beer bottle; I would get one rat, and another would run across the cellar at me."

The hours slogged by slowly. "I watched people's feet from my cellar window," Mother Jones wrote in a letter smuggled out of the dungeon, "miners' feet in old shoes; soldiers' feet, well shod in government leather; the shoes of women with the heels run down; the dilapidated shoes of children; barefooted boys. The children would scrooch down and wave to me, but the soldiers shooed them off."

Mother Jones loved children, and child labor was a fierce rallying point for her.

Today, many young people in the United States have

jobs after school or on weekends, but for most children and teens, their main job is learning in school. One hundred years ago, most children worked just like adults did. Many never got a chance to go to school. At the turn of the twentieth century, 1,750,000 children under age sixteen worked fulltime.[2]

One of the names given to young people in the southern Colorado coal camps was Children of the Coal Shadow. They started school at age four or five and progressed as far as fifth grade before they had to quit. The very lucky ones were able to stay through eighth grade, but seldom beyond that, because the families needed their children's meager incomes. Very few went on to high school. There weren't high schools in the communities owned by the coal companies, so families barely able to feed themselves had to scrounge up a dollar a month, as well as transportation, to send a child to school miles away, in Trinidad or Walsenburg.

More often, girls like Sarah Slator stayed home to help with household chores, such as sweeping the coal soot that constantly settled in their huts and dugouts, hauling water from sluggish streams, and collecting second-rate coal piled at the back of the camp. Some earned a few extra pennies working long hours sewing. And, of course, there were always younger children to care for.

A girl's life wasn't easy, but a boy's was even worse. Preteen boys followed their fathers and grandfathers down into the mines. Some of the boys were so young and so small that their metal lunch buckets scraped the ground as they trudged to work each morning before the sun rose over the Spanish Peaks.

Most boys worked as breakers in the coal mines. Their job was to sift pieces of slate out of the coal that came

Coal mining families needed the small amount of money earned by boys in the mines. Mother Jones fought for increased pay for the men who worked in the coal mines so that their children would not have to work to help their families.

Far underground, trapper boys sat all day and waited to lift the trap door. The upper left corner of the sign reads, "Please don't scare the birds." Why would there be birds in the mines?

tumbling nonstop down a chute. The boys sat on a ladder, shoulders stooped for so many hours a day that it was hard for them to straighten up when their long shift ended. The cascades of coal poured down so fast that many of the boys had their fingers smashed or broken. If a boy got tired or his mind wandered to more pleasant things, such as the baseball games popular with everyone in the camps, the breaker boss would strike the boy's knuckles with a long stick. Blood dribbled and disappeared into the black coal.[3]

Other boys had a less dangerous, but far lonelier job. Those as young as seven or eight worked as **trap boys**. They were stationed in the underground maze of shafts and passageways. Mules deep in the mines pulled cartloads of coal that men had dug out of the cave walls as Mother

Jones said, the trap boys kept "their lone watch in the tombs of the earth with never a human soul to speak to."[4] They waited in the dark, gritty, frigid air until it was time to open and close the trap door for a mule to pass with its weighty load. The mules had shorter workdays and better food than the boys because, as the mine operators often said, humans were cheap and replaceable, while a mule cost $150. Trap boys worked fourteen hours a day for sixty cents, most of the time with their boots sunk in coal mud.

By their early teens, hardworking boys could become mule drivers and eventually advance to **undercutting** and digging coal on their own.

Mother Jones grieved for children whose lives were so bleak. Poor children, such as eleven-year-old Frank Snyder and his brothers and sisters in one of the coal camps, knew they could always find a piece of candy tucked in her pocket. One year, as winter loomed, she brought something more vital to the miners: $500 worth of shoes for children who would otherwise have endured a bitter Colorado winter barefooted.

CHAPTER FIVE

More School, Less Hospital

THE MISSING FINGERS, the ghostly paleness, and the downcast, hopeless eyes of children working in the textile mills and coal mines angered and horrified Mother Jones.

"The employment of children," she said in a speech, "is doing more to fill prisons, insane asylums, almshouses, reformatories, slums and gin shops than all the efforts of reformers are doing to improve society."[1]

She wanted Congress to pass, and President Theodore Roosevelt to sign, a child labor law to be enforced in every state. The law would have required inspections of workplaces and proof of children's ages, so parents could no longer send their children to work at age six or eight.

In order for such a law to wend its way through Congress, people all over the country would have to learn about the conditions under which youngsters worked. They needed to see the children and hear their stories, and then take those stories to their hearts and to their congressmen. Something dramatic had to be done to spread the information.

Mother Jones enjoyed drama. She liked parades, banners, flags, drummers, buglers, costumes, elephants, and, of course, crowds to cheer her speeches. In July 1903, she jumped at the chance to organize the Children's Crusade, a march from Philadelphia to President Roosevelt's summer home in Oyster Bay, New York.

It was, indeed, a spectacle! The ragtag group of four hundred adults and children carried signs that read WE ONLY ASK FOR JUSTICE! Children who had lost fingers and limbs working in the dangerous textile mills waved banners crying out for MORE SCHOOL, LESS HOSPITAL. With Mother Jones at the head of the parade, they trudged on through mud and summer's scorching heat. Each night, Mother Jones gave speeches, and then the children lay down their banners and weary bodies to sleep on the floors of union halls.

President Roosevelt never agreed to meet with them, and so, once they reached his estate, they turned around and headed back. By the time the Children's Crusade returned to Philadelphia in early August, all but forty exhausted marchers had wandered home.

However, the Children's Crusade was a success. It raised national awareness and encouraged states to pass child protection laws or to enforce the laws already on the books. It also led to the formation of a National Child Labor Commission to study conditions and to speak out on behalf of child laborers.

Even so, it wasn't until thirty-five years after the Children's Crusade that the first national law passed to protect children in the workplace. The law said that children below age sixteen were guaranteed a minimum wage of forty cents an hour. They could work no more than forty hours per week and not be allowed to work in hazardous places, such as mills and mines. The minimum age to work in industries classified as hazardous was set at eighteen. Children ages fourteen and fifteen could be employed for limited hours in nonmanufacturing, non-mining, and nonhazardous occupations outside of school hours and during vacations.

No minimum age was set for young people working in agriculture, and the law said nothing about children's wages and conditions in nonhazardous workplaces. Still, it was a major step forward for young laborers.

This landmark law was passed in 1939, nine years after Mother Jones died. She did not live to see the fruits of her labor on behalf of the children she had called "the little gray ghosts."[2]

CHAPTER SIX

Tug-of-War

LABOR DISPUTES WERE COSTLY. How well Mother Jones knew this to be true. During the 1913–1914 Colorado strike, coal production **plummeted**. The railroad had less coal to transport, so it laid off half of its crew.[1] Colorado was forced to squeeze $15 million from its state budget for the expense of dealing with the strike, with months to go before the dispute was settled.[2]

Those sharing the direct, intense stress, however, were the managers and workers. The managers needed to maintain productive factories, mines, railroads, shipyards, and other industries to meet the demand for coal and to make a profit. Mother Jones had no patience for owners and operators driven by huge profits. Her sympathy was always with laborers who needed a safe place to work and a fair wage so they could feed and clothe their families, provide decent shelter, and live with some dignity.

It was a head-on collision of purpose.

Think of a labor dispute as a tug-of-war, with each side furiously pulling a knotted rope to defend its piece of ground. In modern times, members of labor and management sit down at a table and work out their differences, even if it takes weeks or months. If talking doesn't resolve the issues, workers sometimes vote to strike, or walk off their jobs and not return until their demands are met.

Striking families receive financial support from their unions, but the money they receive is not nearly as much as a full salary. Families scrimp and make do, hoping that their sacrifices will pay off in the end when pressure on the industry will force the owners to meet workers' demands or, at least, reach a compromise. Sometimes even a compromise isn't possible, and workers return to their jobs out of desperation.

On the management side, when workers are out on strike, production and service slows down or stops altogether. To keep their businesses running, they sometimes hire new employees to replace the strikers. The striking workers call the new employees **scabs**. Just the image of that word tells the scorn that laborers feel for the strikebreakers.

As in any tug-of-war, there were winners and losers in Mother Jones's many skirmishes. Sometimes the mine owners or factory operators held their position until the workers were forced back to work in grim defeat. Other times, with the aid of unions and Mother Jones's stubborn support, workers returned to slightly safer conditions, shorter hours, and fairer wages.

At times, disputes turned violent. Tempers flared, and tension rose like the mercury in a thermometer on a steamy summer day. Labor and management dug in their heels, neither side willing to give an inch in the tug-of-war. Blood muddied the ground between the two sides.

Mother Jones witnessed and even stirred up her share of bloodshed during strikes. She was jailed dozens of times

In the tug of wars between labor and management, both sides sometimes used firearms.

while organizing unions and urging strikers to stand their ground and keep scabs out of the workplace. "I am against violence, I hate bloodshed, because violence produces violence, and what is won today by violence will be lost tomorrow,"[3] Mother Jones said. Nevertheless, she was also known to advise strikers to stockpile weapons to defend themselves against brutal mine guards. "Buy guns, yes," she said, "and I will borrow money or steal it to buy guns for my boys."[4] In Colorado, she passed out rifles and urged her "boys" to use them.[5]

Mother Jones pulled her weight with high drama. Where there was a labor fight, she dominated center stage, taking her traveling show from border to border, wherever her high-top shoes led her.

CHAPTER SEVEN

Rat Holes

THOSE FAMOUS SHOES TOOK MOTHER JONES from camp to camp to visit mining families and collect verbal ammunition against the mine owners. She dragged her long skirt through the road dust in the dry months and through mud and slush in the wet and cold months. She brought food, medicine, clothes, and shoes, along with a bottomless supply of hope for the despairing mining families. There was hardly a miner, or a miner's wife or child, who didn't recognize and welcome her.

Did the mine operators also recognize her? Yes. Welcome her? Not a bit.

Most coal fields in southern Colorado were owned by one of two companies. The smaller, Victor-American, was concentrated in Huerfano County, with Walsenburg as county seat. In Las Animas County, Colorado Fuel and Iron **(CF&I)** controlled three hundred thousand acres spread out in the foothills of the Spanish Peaks in the Sangre de Cristo mountain range.

CF&I owned every building in its twenty-seven coal mining camps, including the houses—more like clapboard huts—that the miners and their families rented from the company for two dollars per room per month.

One of CF&I's own social workers described these homes as "unfit for the habitation of human beings . . . little removed from the pigsty" and said that some were among the "more repulsive looking rat holes [that] can be found in America."[1] Miners had no choice but to live in "a company shack, the roof of which is so poor that when it rains, the bed is moved from place to place in the attempt to find a dry spot."[2] One miner reported that his family had to huddle under the bed to keep out of the rain.[3]

In addition to monthly rent, the miners paid two dollars a month for coal, thirty-five cents a month for each electrical socket, and a doctor's fee of a dollar a month. The doctor's fee had to be paid, whether or not the family used the medical services. More commonly, mining families treated ailments with their own herbals and remedies brought from their homelands, and they rarely called a doctor for setting bones or delivering babies.[4]

To understand the costs of living in the coal camps, let's say the Snyder family rented a four-room house for mother, father, and their six children. That's eight dollars per month for a shack that most likely had a dirt floor, a leaky roof, a front door hanging by the hinges, and broken windows they'd have to cover with newspapers to keep out wind, dust, and snow.

Add two dollars each month for coal. Maybe they splurged on the luxury of having two electrical sockets. Their rent would be up to ten dollars and seventy cents, and the doctor's fee pushed it to eleven dollars and seventy cents per month. Now consider a miner's average income. In the early 1900s, he made about thirty-one dollars a month.

MONTHLY INCOME AND EXPENSES FOR A FAMILY OF TWO PARENTS, SIX CHILDREN		
The average coal miner in the early 1900s earned $31 per month. This amount is roughly equivalent to $669 per month today, or around $8,000 per year.		
Mandatory Expenses Paid in Scrip to Company	Price	Total Cost
House, 4 rooms	2.00	8.00
Heating and Cooking Coal	2.00	2.00
Electrical sockets, 2	.35	.70
Doctor's fee	1.00	1.00
TOTAL: Mandatory Expenses:		11.70
The balance of **$18.30 per month** paid for other necessities, which were generally purchased at the company store at inflated prices. These included food, medicines, household supplies, blasting powder and lunch buckets for mining work, clothes, shoes, school supplies, and occasional luxuries, such as baseballs or books. What other expenses would a family of eight have?		

After paying those monthly expenses, the Snyder family's disposable income would be about eighteen dollars each month to cover the cost of food, clothes, shoes, basic supplies for the household, medicine, transportation, a small insurance policy, and very modest entertainment. Any hard-earned nickels and dimes to spare went to Mother Jones's work. She had no means of support other than donations and collections at union rallies.[5]

So, what was left after all the bills were paid? A few cents, if they were lucky. In an emergency, such as a husband unable to work because of illness or accident, or a daughter with a burst appendix, there was no money to fall back on.

Illnesses and accidents devastated a family. Miners unable to drag themselves to work went unpaid. There was no such thing as sick leave, paid vacations, or enforceable workers' compensation in the event of an accident on the job.

Fatal accidents were catastrophic for families. Between 1910 and 1913, some 622 children were left fatherless by coal mining accidents in Colorado.[6] Aside from the tragic loss, what would become of families left with no source of income? The meager compensation offered by CF&I barely paid funeral expenses. And with the father no longer working, the family would have to leave the coal camp.

In June 1914, Mother Jones gave a speech in Canada to raise funds to support struggling families in the southern Colorado coal fields. To the Canadian crowd, she said, "I send you a message of the groans and tears of the women and children. Will you relieve them?"[7]

It would take a great deal of relief.

CHAPTER EIGHT

Pluck Me Stores

As Mother Jones knew, coal mining changed the face and pace of America. Southern Colorado coal mines produced mostly soft coals known as lignite and **bituminous coal**. These coals are used for cooking and heating, fueling the railroads, and stoking smelters in steel mills and other industries. Before the nineteenth century, wood was the primary source of fuel. But a good-size pile of coal could supply the same amount of heat as a giant stack of wood, and coal could be transported more economically than wood,[1] without sacrificing trees prized for shade and beauty. By contrast, coal mining was ugly.

"The story of coal," Mother Jones said, "is always the same. It is a dark story."[2]

We've all seen pictures of miners coming out of the caves. They're squinting in the startling light and blackened—sometimes permanently—with coal dust that paints their faces, stains their clothes, seeps into their pores, and embeds itself deep under their fingernails.

"For the privilege of seeing the color of their children's eyes by the light of the sun," Mother Jones continued,

For $1.60 pay per day, coal miners at the time of the Colorado Coal Field Wars dug coal out of the walls for 12 to 14 hours per day.

"fathers must fight as beasts in the jungle."[3] By this she meant the miners worked twelve- to fourteen-hour workdays that included backbreaking "**dead work**," such as hacking at rock, laying track, and fortifying cave walls with timber. This was work a miner was not paid to do. There wasn't any by-the-hour salary. A miner was only paid according to the amount of coal he could dig out of the walls. But this dead work had to be done to get to the coal.

He worked six days a week for his anemic income. His daily take-home of about a dollar and sixty cents was determined by how many tons of coal he dug. The coal a miner cut would be loaded into mule-drawn wagons and weighed by a company **check-weighman**. Quick and often inaccurate, the weighings were sometimes merely guesses, and it was common for a weighman to cheat a miner by underreporting the weight of the coal. The miner had no choice but to accept the weighman's word and swallow his disappointment and anger. If he protested, he could lose his job, and losing his job meant that his family would be evicted from their home. Within three days, all their belongings would be hauled to the side of the road. This was the case with many families Mother Jones met.

Could mining families live on the paltry wages of one dollar and sixty cents per day? Possibly, by supplementing their diet with home gardens, fishing, and hunting wild rabbits and quail—at least, until severe winter forced the vegetables to go to seed and sent the animals into hiding.[4]

Chances are the miners would have lived slightly better if they'd been allowed to shop in town stores. Mine operators made sure that wouldn't happen by paying the men in scrip, which was nothing more than a certificate saying they had the day's wages in credit to be used in company-owned stores. The miners called these "pluck me" stores, as if they were being plucked bare like chickens.

In addition to buying food and day-to-day necessities in these stores, the miners were also required to buy the blasting powder that they used in the mines. Each pay cycle, a miner ended up further in debt to the stores because the prices were hiked up, and when that day's dollar-sixty was converted into spendable cash, it shrank to about a dollar's worth of buying power.

No wonder most mining families finished each month deeper in debt than they were the month before.

Mother Jones told the *New York Times* in June 1913 about a family of five that she literally abducted from the hands of the company store system. The father had been ill for some time, unable to work, and was dying. They'd run up a debt of $30 at the store which, in today's currency, would be about $656. There was no way they'd ever be able to pay off such a debt, and no hope of escaping the burden of the debt until Mother Jones came by night with a wagon and whisked the whole family away. She likened this to helping slaves escape on the Underground Railroad.[5]

Frank Snyder's family had no escape. They were firmly entrenched in the miners' life. So, imagine you are Frank Snyder, and your stomach's rumbling with hunger. Your mother sends you to the company store where the prices are unreasonably high. Of course they would be, because the owners can charge whatever they wish, and you have nowhere else to shop. At the checkout counter you hand over the coal-smudged scrip your father earned that day. A gruff clerk sneers at the dollar-sixty and barks that it will only buy a dollar's worth of bread and milk and meat. If you can put yourself in this scene, then you can understand the soaring sense of injustice building in a miner's family each day.

But, as Mother Jones was fond of saying, "There is no use in our getting discouraged about anything. The storm and sunshine comes and goes, and the fight must still go on."[6]

When Mother Jones visited a coal camp, she would indeed see life going on in its daily grind. She saw the houses built close to the mines. She inhaled the "noxious, foul-smelling gases belching from **coke** ovens,"[7] blown in on the smoggy winds and clouds thick with soot. When the gases and soot settled on the ground, they snuffed out the dream of grass and flowers.

For heating and cooking fuel, someone in the family, usually a daughter, was sent to the **culm bank** at the rear of the camp or colony. A culm bank, also called a slag heap, was a small mountain of forbidding loose rock that had been dumped by the **breaker boys** after the best coal was sorted. Most of the pile was slate and not useful for fuel, so the girl had to rummage around and maybe climb to the top where loose deposits could easily collapse. She could fall right into the heap and even be buried in a black tomb of coal and slate.[8]

Water was fairly plentiful, but not clean. It was muddied by coal slag thick with sulfur, calcium, iron, and camp sewage. It had to be hauled in buckets—sometimes from a burdensome distance—and boiled before use. Naturally, diseases such as typhoid ran rampant because of the overcrowding, poor sanitation, and coal-slag polluted water that were part of the mining families' daily lives.

In many speeches, Mother Jones tugged at hearts and raised tempers describing how a man might crawl through dripping, narrow passages to cut coal, lying on his back in caves too low for him to stand up. If the cave's room were slightly taller, the miner worked bent over for so long that it was too painful for him to straighten his back after his shift ended.[9] Many miners spent their lives with stooped shoulders, even out of the mines. If the cave were tall enough for him to stand, he might have his feet sunk in sulfurous water that ate right through his shoes and bit into his feet.

Given such conditions, it's not surprising that miners suffered all sorts of physical ailments, including burns, broken bones, missing fingers, arthritis, rheumatism, and the dreaded black lung disease.

Black lung was caused by inhaling coal dust over a period of years. Victims of black lung experienced shortness of breath and a persistent, loose cough that often resulted in spitting vile black mucous.[10] In the early 1900s, no one knew that better ventilation and face masks would help to prevent this debilitating disease, which was later identified as pneumoconiosis. It wasn't until 1969 that Congress passed the Coal Mine Health and Safety Act to prevent, diagnose, and treat the condition. At the same time, Congress established the Black Lung Disability Trust to compensate miners who got this disabling disease or their widows. And yet, as recently as 2010, a report was released that three men die each day of this disease.[11]

CHAPTER NINE

Roaring Whirling of Flaming Air

LIKE THE TRUE SHOWMAN SHE WAS, Mother Jones had quirky disguises she wore to spy unnoticed in textile mills and coal camps. In Pennsylvania, she masqueraded as a missionary and met with mill workers to knit mittens to send to Africa.[1] This way, she was able to **infiltrate** the textile industry, as she did in several southern states, and gather firsthand evidence of the working conditions and the mill operators' strategies.[2]

She once disguised herself as a peddler selling needles and small household necessities. She hid her stout and dour black-gowned self in a peasant's calico dress, and tucked her white fluffy hair under a wide sunbonnet. Dressed this way, she moved freely through the coal camps without attracting the attention of the mine operators.[3]

Once she was within the walls of a miner's home—even if that home was a canvas tent during a strike—she'd drop her disguise and go back to her real identity. She'd take some time to bounce a baby on knees that were beginning to protest the seventy thousand miles she'd covered in her vagabond career.[4] Many nights she trekked eight to ten miles up and down the mountains in West Virginia,[5] or slogged across riverbeds and ravines, or tramped along railroad tracks and through banked snow and black slush.

Not all of her wanderings were done on foot, as in this description of a 1901 meeting with miners in West Virginia: "We were up the mountain at S Caperton last night and came down the goat path after 12 o'clock. I had to slide down most of it. My bones are all sore today."[6] If only someone had thought to take a picture of Mother Jones with her black gown billowing around her as she slid down the goat path!

She also claimed that she'd slipped unnoticed into the coal mines to check on conditions inside and dig a bit of coal herself. It's unlikely that such a mischievous deed occurred. She could not have disguised herself well enough to fool the miners who had a deep superstition that women in the mines caused bad luck. There are a few reports of women in European mines, but in the United States, women went no deeper than the mouths of the mines. The mere suggestion of a woman inside a mine shaft was a sure omen of disaster for the camp.

Miners and their wives harbored other superstitions. Some thought that their dreams and images foretold disaster and were compelling reasons not to go to work the next day. Accidents in the mines were common, and mining posed the most severe injuries of any industry in the early 1900s. Colorado had twice the rate of coal mine deaths than anywhere else in America.[7,8] Each day threatened disaster, ranging from oxygen deprivation to fire or explosions to the collapse of cave roofs and walls.

Runaway mine cars and exposed electric wires led to many accidents, as did faulty lifts that carried miners deep into the earth. There was only one way in and out. It wasn't until well into the twentieth century that mine operators were required to provide double escape shafts; even then, they rarely complied. Also, a miner working a narrow passage might be crushed between a mule-pulled car loaded with tons of coal and the very wall from which that coal had been dug.

Poor ventilation in the mines worsened "**damps**," which were gases such as methane trapped in pockets within the rock, sometimes building to intense powder-keg pressure. Carbonic acid gas, called black damp, referred to atmosphere that held little oxygen. Miners dreaded damps. Without enough breathable oxygen, they experienced numbness, joint pain, headaches, a drumming sound in their ears, choking, and slow death. Miners used to "brush the roof," meaning they'd wave their shirts above their heads to beat away the noxious gases, but this was ineffective. Sometimes, suspended dust or leaking damps would ignite, causing fires or explosions. Escape was unlikely. The lucky victims died immediately, while some of their coworkers slowly suffocated from carbon monoxide gas generated by the explosion.

In Priscilla Long's fascinating book, *Where the Sun Never Shines*, she offers a dramatic description of a mine explosion.[9] The first sign is a loud thunderclap. Then the cave is illuminated with brilliant lightning, a "roaring whirling of flaming air," which destroys everything in its path. It "wastes its volcanic fury in a discharge of thick clouds of coal dust, stones, and timber." One survivor of such an explosion described a river of fire passing over him.

Crushing cave-ins could be just as devastating. Miners listened for a sound like thunder over their heads, indicating that the upper layers were "working," meaning that the timbers supporting the roof or walls were splitting, and the roof was about to collapse. While it made sense for miners to get out as soon as they heard this ominous sound, they also knew that it could take two or three days for the roof to cave in—two or three days during which they could be earning their meager wage. Many wished they'd heeded the warning signs earlier.

Coal mines were often overrun with rats and mice that feasted on the oats intended for the mules. Some of the miners adopted the rodents as friendly companions in the lonely caves, even sharing their lunch so often that their "pets" came sniffing around for treats on a regular basis.

More commonly, miners watched the rats for signs of danger. When the rats stampeded, the men followed them out as quickly as possible. They trusted the rodents' exquisite hearing to predict a cave-in. Others were not wise enough to trust the rats.

In the 1910s, the average life expectancy was fifty years, compared to seventy-eight in the 2010s. Widows of miners loitered around coal camps in hopes of landing a new husband to support their children. Likewise, since women often died in childbirth or succumbed to influenza or typhoid fever, their husbands were desperate to find new wives to care for children left behind.

Colorado had a law requiring mine owners to compensate a miner's widow. However, the law only applied when the company was at fault. The reality was that coroners, judges, and juries were under the control of mine owners and found it in their own best interests not to declare the companies at fault. In short, there were families that simply starved or split apart, with the children sent elsewhere to survive, even to orphanages.

Mother Jones called these mine owners pirates, high-class burglars, and other far less polite names.

Mine cave-ins were one of many dangers that miners faced every workday.

CHAPTER TEN

Hit 'Em Again, Mother Jones!

MINING FAMILIES CLUNG TO GHOST STORIES about dead men trapped within the dark mines and never brought to the surface. Their eerie spirits were said to haunt the caves forever. But mining families were haunted daily in a much more realistic way. Frantic wives waited at home wondering if they'd be widows by dark.

As each miner emerged at the end of his shift, he would hang his numbered brass tag on a board. A gap on the board, a missing number, meant tragedy and provided a grim way of identifying the dead, especially when bodies were burned beyond recognition in an explosion.

Frank Snyder's family seemed blessed. All six children were healthy. Frank was the firstborn and, at age eleven, was certainly old enough to go down into the mines to work. Many trapper boys were as young as seven or eight, but Frank did not yet work the mines as his father did.

Each night Frank and his brothers and sisters waited anxiously until they knew that their father had hung his numbered tag on the name board after his shift and would come safely home for a hot bath and supper.

Of those husbands and fathers who did not come home, Mother Jones would say, "Pray for the dead and fight like hell for the living."[1]

Twelve years before what would come to be known as the Ludlow **Massacre**, Mother Jones made a landmark speech at a convention of the United Mine Workers **(UMW)**. Seldom were women allowed to speak at such gatherings. She would often try to get a permit to hold a meeting, but would be denied. One of those times, the man in charge had said, "Mother Jones, you can't talk." She laughed and replied, "For God's sake, did you ever see a woman that couldn't talk?"[2]

And talk she did at that 1902 UMW convention, where she excited and incited the crowd with these words:

"Things are happening today that would have aroused our Revolutionary fathers in their graves. People sleep quietly, but it is the sleep of the slave chained closely to his master. If this generation surrenders its liberties, then the work of our forefathers . . . will not be resurrected for two generations to come."[3]

She spoke of the brutality of mine guards. She reminded the miners in the audience of how those who joined the union might be thrown into "the bullpen." The bullpen was a primitive stockade where miners could be held indefinitely and therefore unable to work for his $1.60 a day. Or they might be forced like slaves onto chain gangs in temperatures that fell to forty degrees below zero. Or they might be taken to "the kangaroo," which was a code name for a spot where an uncooperative miner or labor agitator would be beaten. Even worse, Mother Jones reminded them that union men could be sent "**down the canyon**," meaning they'd be blacklisted from being hired in any of the mines, and their families would surely starve.[4]

Mother Jones's nemesis, Brigadier General John Chase, the man who kept banishing Mother Jones or confining her to jail, swore that her only goal was to stir up "the more ignorant and criminally disposed to deeds of violence and crime."[5]

While this statement shows little respect for the miners and their families, it does point out that Mother Jones sometimes used questionable methods.

In fact, her life exemplified the idea that the end justifies the means. In other words, she would do whatever was necessary in the fight for laborers' benefits. Mother Jones had a "tendency to play fast and loose with fact."[6] To rally the labor troops, she used every weapon in her arsenal, including fear, intimidation, insults, biblical quotes and misquotes, prayer, sentimentality, threats, lies, humiliation, false hope, and promises she often could not keep.

But as soon as someone hoisted her up on a tree stump or a table to speak, hearts pounded. People stomped their feet and pumped the air; they whooped and hollered and shouted responses, such as, "Hit 'em again, Mother Jones! Tell it to 'em again!"[7]

She did. As the late August 1913 weather began to hint of winter, tensions between the miners and the mine operators, primarily Victor-America and CF&I, heated to boiling in Colorado. Mother Jones issued the alarm in whining wails and resounding blasts. Men, women, and children ripe for change opened their drowsy eyes, spurred on to union action.

In that year, Ludlow's fate was sealed. The Great Colorado Coal Field War was about to explode.

CHAPTER ELEVEN

Slavery or Strike

THE GREAT COLORADO COAL FIELD WAR was the major southern Colorado coal mining strike in 1913–1914, and Mother Jones was there. It certainly wasn't her first such labor fight in the state. Ten years earlier, she had helped organize miners in strikes that spanned a good portion of Colorado, north to south. Those earlier strikes were fairly peaceful, though not very successful in getting better working conditions for the miners.

Now, after ten more years of grinding poverty and unrest, miners were near the breaking point. Because of the tireless campaigning of Mother Jones and United Mine Workers organizers, the UMW union had gained strength, but only through secret membership. As Mother Jones was fond of saying, the "servile lick-spittle authorities forbade all assembly."[1] Miners could be jailed, beaten, or fired if they were known to be union members or if they even talked to one another about union business and uniting for better working conditions. CF&I hired "hoboes, thugs, ex-convicts, and gunmen" as guards, spies, and enforcers of this rule.[2]

At a miners' convention in Trinidad in mid-September 1913, not all of the miners dared to show up to hear

Mother Jones's speech, which was later described as the spirit of revolt. It reached an ear-splitting frenzy, after which the union voted unanimously to go out on strike. Mother Jones threw out the challenge: "It is up to you, my boys, to gain victory!"[3]

Even though they were downtrodden, miners and their wives were often hesitant to show up to hear her speeches. Mother Jones relished telling about a certain outdoor meeting of small-town West Virginia miners. It was unlikely that she'd be able to assemble a crowd, as miners were afraid to show up for fear of losing their jobs. She seated herself on a rock in a woodsy clearing and waited. With "smiling eyes," (her words) she watched her wary audience climb one-by-one up through mountain passes and hide behind huge boulders or trees. Women were "lurking in the thickets." Her hidden audience peeked around their cover as she began to speak their universal language.[4]

Often the miners and their wives absorbed her revolutionary words at secret meetings like those held in clearings in the woods of West Virginia. Many a night, after the miners had washed off the coal dust that ground into their pores and under their nails, they would drag their weary bodies to wherever Mother Jones was speaking and seize her strength and will as their own. Mine operators were sometimes aware of these clandestine gatherings. They sent spies to take notes that were sent to state officials, including Colorado Governor Elias Ammons.[5]

Imagine eleven-year-old Frank Snyder present at one of Mother Jones's blast of oratory in such a clearing on a cool fall night:

Excitement and rage ripple through him in the night air as he watches Mother Jones balance her fireplug body and plant her scuffed high-top shoes up on a tree stump. She pulls the long pins out of her hat and throws them into the crowd. Smoothing down her white hair and her shawl, she thrusts a palm toward the crowd in a command for silence.[6]

Frank waits with the others, in hushed anticipation. Mother Jones's eyes slowly scan the crowd, and even though there are a thousand people with their faces turned up to hers, Frank is sure those piercing blue eyes are drilling right into his own.

She rouses the audience exhausted from a day's backbreaking work:

"Injustice boils in men's hearts as does steel in its cauldron, ready to pour forth, white hot, in the fullness of time."[7]

She offers motherly advice to strengthen the miners' moral fiber:

"Young men, let me say to you, keep away from the saloon, the pool room, the gambling den. There is nothing for you in them. Develop your brain and heart by serving humanity and reading human history."[8]

Well, sure, Frank agrees, but his father hasn't got any spare time at the end of the workday to read human history. His dad can barely find the energy to read a newspaper in the camp's social hall. Sometimes he falls asleep soaking in the galvanized tub that takes up most of the kitchen.

And then, Mother Jones shifts her maternal stance and revs up to feed the anger and shame of the crowd. Frank reddens with embarrassment for his father.

"You great strong men have been enslaved for years. You have allowed a few men to boss you, to starve you, to abuse your women and children, to deny you education.… What is the matter with you? Are you afraid? Do you fear your pitiful little bosses?… I can't believe you are so cowardly, and I tell you this, if you are, you are not fit to have women live with you."[9]

The wives and mothers in the crowd smirk. The husbands and fathers bristle with shame and ease away from the sharp jabs of their wives' elbows.

The only solution to the many woes of mining families, Mother Jones preaches, is to join the union, even if it has to be done on the sly, behind the backs of the mine guards and spies.

The crowd stirs. Sarah Slator is there in the crowd, no doubt, along with all the other older children. They all need a shot of Mother Jones's determination to face the hungry days ahead.

Frank senses a resolve rising from the ground beneath him.

Mother Jones shouts louder. Join the union. Organize, demand changes, stand fast. And if the actions of reasonable men fail, well then, you show those thugs, those pirates and high-class burglars.

"If it is strike or submit, why, for God's sake, strike! Strike until you win!"[10]

Mother Jones's words pound all of them like a sudden summer storm.

"We are going to stay here in Southern Colorado until the banner of industrial freedom floats over every coal mine. We are going to stand together and never surrender."[11]

Wild applause sends leaves fluttering to the ground and nearly drowns out her words, until she raises her clenched fists in the air and shouts,

"Rise up and strike! If it is slavery or strike, I say strike until the last one of you drop into your graves."[12]

Frank waves his arms in the air; it feels like the revival meeting he'd once been to. Surprising himself, he shouts out his fury in solidarity with a thousand other voices.

Mother Jones lets the righteous fury and resolve thunder through the forest a good, long while. Finally, the mother of the entire family of labor eases her children back into their workaday world with calm reassurance.

"Boys, let Mother tell you one thing. Freedom is not dead. She is only gently resting. She is sleeping quietly, waiting only for you to call."[13]

On September 23, 1913, the miners called, loud and clear.

CHAPTER TWELVE

Strike!

On that September day, a bold group of men put their futures and their families at risk by presenting the mine operators with a list of their demands that included:

- the right to form and join a union to represent them in collective bargaining
- an increase in wages, to be paid in real money, not scrip
- enforcement of the eight-hour workday law, which was generally ignored
- pay for necessary mine work ("dead work") that did not directly result in carloads of coal
- the election of check-weighmen by the miners instead of their being appointed by the mine operators
- the right to trade in any store and choose doctors
- the elimination of the brutal guard system

The mine operators, who represented the mine owners such as John D. Rockefeller Jr. of CF&I and Jay Gould of Victor-American, flatly refused to consider the demands.

" 'Tis an outrage," Mother Jones would say, "that Rockefeller should own the coal that God put in the earth for *all* people."[1] Her comment was one of a long, knotty string of radical statements that went beyond demands for better treatment of miners. She was also on a quest to nationalize coal mining. Nationalized coal mining would mean that the operation of coal mines would be in the hands of the federal government. Mother Jones believed that only in this way would miners be treated with justice and coal be cheap and available to all Americans, and not be controlled by the men she called rich coal barons. Not only that, she proclaimed, but the conflict between labor and capital would not end until the United States took over *all* industries. She fully believed that such a thing would happen.[2]

However, it did not happen in the coal industry then or later, and miners continued to be subjected to the whims and injustices of mine operators.

At the end of the work day on September 23, 1913, frustrated and furious, the miners laid down their picks and hammers, their drills and shovels, their methane-testing lamps and their **carbide lamps**, and they declared a general strike. Sweat mixed with black coal dust and caked their skin. Their metal lunch buckets emptied of the two meals they'd eaten in the dim glow of their helmet lights now clanged against the wobbly basket elevator that carried them thousands of feet to the surface. Those men whom Mother Jones called the slaves of the caves now burned with hope and determination.

Squinting in the golden autumn light, they marched out of the dark caves.

They did not go back for fifteen months that were miserable for the miners and their families, and miserable for the mine owners and their operators.

Perhaps the only ones happy about the strike, besides Mother Jones, were the legendary canaries that were often released into the caves to test for deadly methane gas. The mules enjoyed a lengthy vacation, and the cave rats went hungry.

The work stoppage did not mean that the miners would enjoy a nice, long holiday. It meant that everything changed for the family. Remember, in the early twentieth century, men who worked in the southern Colorado mines lived in houses owned by the company that ran the mines. They shopped in stores, attended schools, visited doctors, and went to churches all provided by the owners. When miners refused to go back to the mines, the owners took their own kind of action: they gave a mining family three days to move out of their house.

But where would these families go? How would they find a new home? How would they get money for fuel and food? Where would the children go to school or play safely? What if someone in the family got very sick?

Parents tried to reassure their children, but the days ahead were sure to be riddled with troubling uncertainties.

CHAPTER THIRTEEN

Exodus of Woe

AN EARLY FROST CHILLED THE FAMILIES of some eleven thousand miners—about 90 percent of all workers in the southern Colorado mines—as they gathered their ragged clothes and splintered furniture and mismatched belongings to prepare for their move. The weather worsened in a torrential rain, then a blinding blizzard, then sleet, unusual for so early in the fall. As temperatures dropped and ice blanketed the ground and frosted the distant mountain peaks, families were forced at rifle point to leave coal company property.[1]

Boys like Frank Snyder did whatever they could to ease the burden of the move on their mothers. The younger children were confused and frightened, seeking warmth in their mothers' arms as their fathers loaded all their belongings on a wagon.

Wheels of overloaded wagons sank into the slushy mud. "Out of the canyons and across prairie flats crept long lines of pushcarts and mule wagons carrying unsmiling families."[2] Men hauled the wagons; women pushed them. Small children rode on top of the heaps.

Mother Jones had encouraged the strikers with her

confidence and promises. Shortly before the strike began, she'd said, "Let the fight go on. ... If nobody else will keep on, I will."[3] But she had business elsewhere, perhaps in Texas, and was not rain-drenched along with them on their trek. In temperatures punishingly cold, homeless single men and families like Frank Snyder's and Sarah Slator's made the long march to one of the thirteen tent colonies that the United Mine Workers were setting up for them.

How hard it must have been for Frank's family of eight to face the uncertainties ahead. Their wagon tottered with the mountainous load and inched through mud ruts, all their possessions exposed to the ravages of the weather. Trudging the miles, they had to negotiate the rain and slush, and there was no guarantee that tomorrow would be any better—if they didn't all freeze to death during the first night.

The *Denver Express* described the scene as "an exodus of woe, of a people leaving known fears for new terrors, a hopeless people seeking new hope ... a people born to suffering going forth to new suffering."[4]

The southern Colorado coal field encompassed some forty miles in and out of the deep-cut canyons from Walsenberg to Trinidad. Makeshift tent colonies were hastily set up along the route for access to the coal seam entrances. While a few of the displaced families slept on the floors of union halls or camped in the homes of strike sympathizers on their way to their tent homes, most weathered the storm by huddling under their wagons, with little more than blankets to shield them.

Ludlow was the largest of the tent colonies and home to striking families, most of whom were evicted from their company-owned houses in Tabasco and Berwind canyons. Ludlow's advantage was its strategic location close to the mine entrances and also close to the railroad spur. The railroad location was key both for ease of transportation and for stopping immigrant strikebreakers as they left the train, keeping them from reaching the mines. But when the frozen and exhausted families reached Ludlow, most having traveled on foot four or five miles from their former homes, there were no tents set up to house them. The railroad had lost the tents that the union had shipped.

There was, however, a cheerful reception committee at Ludlow. Mary Thomas, the fiery, redheaded, five-foot-tall Welsh soprano, was barely twenty-two and already the mother of Olga and Rachael, ages three and five, when Ludlow Tent Colony dotted the prairie. She'd come to Colorado with her girls to track down her miner husband and get him to support the family. The wickedly outspoken Mary found him, but the scoundrel again abandoned the family shortly after Ludlow Tent Colony opened.[5]

Nevertheless, Mary and her children stayed on. She appointed herself official greeter for the shivering and weary newcomers, helping to organize preparation of the many meals that had to be cooked on the few stoves in working order. She made it her mission to pull the varied ethnic groups together into a community. She also took it upon herself to convince the women, hungry and freezing and frightened, not to let their husbands go back to work until their union demands were met.

The lost tents resurfaced somewhere on the railroad route four days later.[6] Two hundred tents soon became home to about twelve hundred residents, half of whom were women and children[7] and all of whom were surrounded by unfriendly mine guards.

"I hope there is no war in Trinidad," Mother Jones had said, referring to all the coal fields around Trinidad, "for it will cause suffering. But if the war has to be made that the boys in the mines may have their rights—let it come!"[8]

It came. By the end of it, dozens of men, women, and children were injured or dead on both sides in one of the bloodiest labor wars on record.

CHAPTER FOURTEEN

Ducking Gunfire September/October 1913

BLOOD WAS SPILLED FROM THE FIRST DAY OF THE STRIKE. A miner at Segundo colony died, apparently shot by a mine guard.[1] At another colony, a boy fell dead with nine bullet holes in his leg. Both sides of the conflict were heavily armed for battle. Ludlow alone boasted of some forty guns—rifles, shotguns, and revolvers—and this number quadrupled within a few months as the warfare mounted.

The United Mine Workers established Ludlow, the largest of the tent colonies, as a military site because it was strategically located a half mile from the Ludlow train depot. Each Ludlow miner was issued a red bandana as his uniform in the war, and "rednecks"* were posted as guards on the outskirts of Ludlow colony day and night.

The mine owners' detectives, some wearing sheriff badges and fighting like soldiers, rolled in an armored

*The term *redneck* has a different meaning here from its later use as a disapproving term for a rural white Southerner.

vehicle that the strikers called the Death Special. It had bulletproof sides and a Gatling machine gun mounted on its top. The Death Special soldiers roamed the countryside from one tent colony to the next, making sport of spraying machine gunfire over the tops of the strikers' tents.[2]

Mother Jones later testified about a conversation she'd had in October with a railroad man. It's unclear if he had overheard or intercepted secret orders from the militia aboard a train, but he had burst into her hotel room with a dire message:

"My God, Mother," he said, "they are going to clean up the miners and the tents . . . the gunmen, they are going to murder them all!"[3]

While the *Trinidad Chronicle-News* was advertising a mysterious substance called "oriental cream or magical beautifier, guaranteed to remove pimples, freckles, and moth patches,"[4] the miners' families had much more

Guns were available to both sides in the Colorado Coal Field War, but the forces hired by the mine operators and owners were better armed. The striking miners called this armored vehicle 'the Death Special.'

serious issues to deal with than blemishes. Ducking gunfire, they were attempting to set up households and settle into something resembling normal life. The tent walls were supported by dangerously thin slats of lumber. Wood planks over the frozen earth served as floors. Women used stoves sent from Illinois or cooked outdoors over open fires. There was ample heating coal and water available, though the water had to be hauled in buckets from a pump house near the railroad tracks. For some of the tents, the trek to water might be a mile.[5]

Hygiene was a different matter. Trenches were dug around the perimeter of the colony for outhouses, but when temperatures fell to fifty degrees below zero, most people relieved themselves in chamber pots in their tents.

Besides the physical hardships, hunger and money were enormous issues. The union, stretched to its limits after two decades of contentious strikes, provided a small stipend for each miner. Peering again over the shoulder of Frank Snyder, we can see how his family would have suffered. Every two weeks, a miner and his wife received two dollars and fifty cents from the union and thirty-five cents for each child.[6] For the Snyders, who had six children, that would total four dollars and sixty cents. But they had been used to receiving nine dollars and sixty cents every week.

What could four dollars and sixty cents every two weeks buy for two parents and six hungry children? Not much. Like everyone else in Ludlow, the Snyders went without.

What would Mother Jones have seen and heard had she been in Ludlow Tent Colony? People of thirty nationalities or ethnic groups had segregated themselves into little colonies. They spoke at least twenty-seven different languages plus a sort of **pidgin** English that enabled them to communicate across language barriers. In addition to immigrants from southern and eastern Europe, the colony was home to Asians, Mexicans, American Hispanics, and African Americans, as well as white Americans, such as Frank Snyder's family.

The Greeks were perhaps the best organized ethnic group at Ludlow, often operating boardinghouse tents for single men. The Greeks referred to all other ethnicities in the colony as "foreigners." Their leader was a young man named Anastasios Spantidakis.[7] He was known as Louis Tikas to the rest of the colony. Because of his leadership gifts and his comfort with the English language, he fell into the position as second-in-command at Ludlow, behind John Lawson, the union leader.

Tikas was a charming man, perhaps twenty-five years old and noted for wearing a sporty motoring hat and puttees, which were strips of cloth wrapped from ankle to knee. He'd come to America to dig coal, and he quickly became a calming influence for the single Greek men there, who were known to be hotheaded and ripe for battle. Tikas may have been attended college before he came to the United States. He was bright, articulate, and fair-minded. All of these qualities made him the ideal liaison between the Greeks and the larger community, and between the entire colony and the militia, as tensions in the coal fields grew. The miners' hope was that Tikas might be able to negotiate a nonviolent solution to the standoff between the two sides.

The Trinidad Free Press dubbed him "Louis the Greek … mayor and guardian angel of the little tented colony at Ludlow."[8] To his countrymen in Ludlow, he was *strategos* (the general), and they affectionately called him "our brave General Tikas." So important was he to the Ludlow community that he was allowed to move out of the bachelor tent and into a nicer location: a tent near the baseball diamond. There in privacy, he enjoyed use of the most valuable piece of technology in the camp—a telephone, which he later used to keep communication open with enemy officers.

Tikas began having his meals in the tent of his neighbor, Pearl Jolly, the camp nurse. Pearl was twenty and had been married for a year. Nothing is known of Pearl's husband, except that he was a Scot. People said that Pearl and Louis were "keeping company" and that they'd slipped away from

Because their houses were owned by the coal company, striking coal miners and their families were forced to move into tent colonies.

the colony more than once to go dancing in town. Rumor had it that an underground passage led from Louis's tent to Pearl's. None was needed, they protested, as their tents were so close.

Pearl Jolly was daring and liked taking risks. When the Colorado National Guard was called in to end the strike, Pearl mobilized the women into a "mop and broom brigade" and led them in jeering and taunting the militia and the strikebreakers.

There were those who didn't much like Pearl. Mary Thomas, arguably her rival for most eccentric resident, said that Pearl was one of a kind who forced herself on everybody. Pearl's pushiness served the colony well on that terrible Monday, April 20, when she and Tikas became heroes of a bloody encounter.

CHAPTER FIFTEEN

Baseball and the Bloomer Girls

RACIAL AND ETHNIC CONFLICTS WERE SURE TO FLARE with such a diversity of poor, hardscrabble people in one small community. Japanese immigrants were not welcome, since so many unknowingly came as scabs and had little in common with other groups' languages, cultures, or religions. The embers of ethnic strife were fanned by the mine operators, who believed that the more tension that flared among the diverse groups, the less likely it was that the whole colony would unite against the mine owners. There was much at stake for the mine owners, since the multicultural miners "tore 100,000 tons of coal every year from each of the twenty-two big mines in the Trinidad coalfield."[1]

Yet the melting pot of nationalities at Ludlow quickly evolved into a true community. Helen Ring Robinson, a Colorado state senator sympathetic to the plight of the workers, visited Ludlow frequently and reported on the reduction in ethnic strife, particularly among the women. She wondered if the women's cooperative spirit reflected their belief that they had more to win in the strike than the men did.[2]

Despite the melting pot atmosphere, leaders were elected for each national or ethnic group and for the colony itself, to maintain order and plan events. A large tent flying an American flag contained a stage for meetings and social celebrations. Another giant tent served as the

Families from diverse backgrounds went on strike together at Ludlow and lived in the tent colony.

school. And, of course, a baseball diamond was marked out. What would camp life be without baseball?

Nothing was more popular with all ages than baseball. Each camp had a squad or two that competed against the teams at other camps. One camp reportedly fielded an all-female team dubbed the Bloomer Girls. If Mother Jones had looked more closely, she would have seen that there were actually only two females on the team. All the rest were men wearing wigs.[3]

Even though some of the mine guards played on the camp baseball teams, as a group the guards and unruly detectives did their best to make the tent dwellers miserable. One technique was to sweep high-powered searchlights back and forth over the colony all night so people couldn't sleep. One redneck solved that problem by borrowing a powerful rifle from a Trinidad dentist to shoot out a searchlight.[4]

Striking families struggled to avoid gunfire, frostbite, and hunger during that bitter winter. Mother Jones visited the residents in October and encouraged them as they made do with very little. She would have seen injustices, but she also would have witnessed that life was not all gloom and doom in Ludlow, especially as ethnic tensions eased into a community united in a shared sense of purpose.

There were daytime classes for children and night school for adults to learn English, American civics and values, personal hygiene, and home economics. There were youth clubs with games, dramas, and contests, as well as adult social clubs. Lodges, subgroups within the union, formed along ethnic lines for companionship and modest insurance benefits. There were lending libraries, lecturers, and churches.

Nearly every Saturday, miners and their wives and teenage children forgot their woes and danced well into the night, swinging their partners to bands from Walsenburg and Trinidad that played music from all over the world for homesick immigrants. The raucous music also provided cover for people who wanted to discuss union business, since such talk was forbidden by the mine owners.[5]

Religion enriched the lives of many of the miners, who often brought their religious beliefs and customs from their homelands. The predominant religions were Catholicism and Eastern Orthodox Christianity. The pre-strike mining camps had small churches, though they were under the influence of the mine operators who chose and hired the clergy. This way, management further controlled any potential political and social issues that might arise in the lives of the laborers. The operators "kept the church on a short leash."[6]

Religious practice was hard to sustain in the tent colonies. Some miners made the difficult trip into the towns of Trinidad or Walsenburg to attend church. They sometimes had to wait for priests to marry and bury the colonists. Infant mortality was high, and for the deeply faithful, the desire for a proper burial service was intense. Often women performed baptisms for their neighbors' babies, and men performed funeral rites.

Rock-drilling contests provided healthy competition and gambling opportunities. Mining camps, and later tent colonies, trained their own drillers and chose the fastest among them to compete against men from rival camps on the Fourth of July. In some years, the winners went to Denver for the state finals at the annual Festival of Mountain and Plain. These champs trained for weeks after work, preparing themselves for the punishing ordeal of wielding jackhammers for fifteen minutes, non-stop, in one-man or two-man feats. The payoffs were well worth the effort. In those fifteen minutes, a champion two-man team could drill a hole thirty-five inches deep in thick granite, and ride home victorious with a prize of $5,000.[7]

Such competitions, along with baseball, dances, dramas, literary circles, and spirited children's games helped to ease the miners and their families through the long, desperate strike.

CHAPTER SIXTEEN

Scabs
September/October 1913

WHERE WAS MOTHER JONES, the most prominent and visible woman in the labor movement, during those early months of the strike? In jail a good bit of the time. Though she was welcome in the camps and tents, she was not greeted warmly by mine operators, hired guards, and militiamen who spied on her secret meetings in the woods or witnessed her firebrand speeches at the mouths of mines. It was no secret that they had their crosshairs on Mother Jones.

Shortly before the strike began in September 1913, she wrote a letter to an old friend named Terence Powderly in which she said, "They are sending me all sorts of threats here [in Trinidad]. They have my skull drawn on a picture and two cross sticks underneath my jaw to tell me that if I do not quit, they are going to get me. Well, they've been a long time at it."[1]

Of course, Mother Jones was no stranger to jail cells. She had been arrested banished, or locked up dozens of times across the country. At one time, she was even convicted of murder, although the charges were dropped. She once described being in a West Virginia jail where she was "lodged with murderers and thieves, but who to me were much more civilized than the coal barons."[2] She also said, "If they want to hang me, let them hang me. But when I am on the scaffold, I'll cry, 'Freedom for the working class!' "[3]

With such words, she provoked arrests, and each new arrest brought publicity to the labor unions. During her notorious battles with the Colorado State Militia and its commander, General Chase, she said, "Chase will throw me in jail.... He'll do it because he doesn't know that persecution always helps instead of hinders any battle."[4] In fact, when she was whisked off to jail in one of those new inventions, the automobile, strikers lined the streets waving and cheering, eager for the next public protest. Her influence did not fade. Triumphantly, she wielded even more power from her prison cells.

General John Chase commanded the Colorado State Militia during the Ludlow strike. He arrested Mother Jones several times.

She had left her footprint on many states and towns. But when she left it on southern Colorado, she stomped hard on the state. Once the strike began in September, she organized numerous protests and parades. In October, four thousand strikers from all over the state poured into Trinidad by rail, by wagon, and on foot. Mother Jones enlisted a rousing band and led a mob of furious women with children in tow. She shrewdly placed children at the front of the demonstration, waving banners that read A BUNCH OF MOTHER JONES'S CHILDREN and WE WANT FREEDOM, NOT CORPORATION RULES. Their mission was to confront Governor Elias Ammons, who was in Trinidad. The governor huddled behind closed doors and refused to see the marchers.

"Unlock this door and come out here," Mother Jones yelled, pounding on the governor's hotel room door. "These women ain't going to bite you."[5]

Such bravado on her part did not endear her to the governor, who, she once said, should be hanged. He responded by calling out the state militia to replace the mob of mine guards and hired thugs. Striking miners welcomed the Colorado National Guard with great enthusiasm, a band, and waving banners. They were assured that the militia would be impartial peacekeepers.

General Chase, however, had nothing but contempt for the union and its ardent organizers. He led his men in his own way, causing a bigger split between the two sides of the conflict. Gun warfare escalated. Chase ordered the strikers to surrender their guns and apparently expected to get hundreds. What he got were thirty-seven rusting rifles and one child's popgun.[6]

With coal production down, mine operators recruited laborers by using false advertising throughout the United

States, Europe, Asia, and Mexico. That was how most of the Japanese immigrants found their way across the Pacific to the Rocky Mountains. They, and workers of other nationalities, were promised steady jobs. What was not mentioned in the ads was that these newcomers would be scabs. In September 1902, the *New York Times* wrote, "Like a plague the word 'scab' carries terror into every working-man's home."[7] Clearly, strikebreakers were detested and considered traitors by the mining families struggling through a bitter strike and one of the worst winters in Colorado history.

Miners took their anger out on the scabs. The state militia was under orders to stop intimidation of those miners who were willing to work despite the strike by escorting them safely to the mines.[8] This was not a simple task. The strikers and their families got into the act with every makeshift weapon at their disposal. As a result, the strikebreakers were protected, while strikers were randomly arrested and herded into bullpens where they would be kept without charges against them until General Chase decided to let them out.

Gradually, some of the immigrant strikebreakers began to understand that they'd been misled, driven by their own hunger. They tried to leave the coal fields. Quickly, the role of the militia evolved into forcing the scabs to stay and work. Imagine the confusion of men who were new in a country far from home, many illiterate, and most knowing only a few words of English. They had been told they had to pay off their railroad fare and room and board, according to contracts they'd been blindsided into signing, sometimes under the influence of free whiskey. At one mine camp, guards took away the strikebreakers' shoes so they couldn't escape. Many drifted off anyway, ending up at Ludlow under the protective wing of Louis Tikas, the leader of the Greek community.

Mother Jones made her sentiments known about scabs. Well into the strike, she journeyed to El Paso, Texas, to try and halt the flow of Mexican workers into the Colorado coal fields. After an hour or two of talking with Mexican revolutionary hero Pancho Villa, an agreement was reached: no more Mexican strikebreakers went to Trinidad.[9]

Mother Jones traveled to Washington, D.C., to demand a congressional investigation into the militia's conduct during the strike, then hurried back to Denver to lead yet another demonstration on December 16. There, two thousand people demanded to speak to the governor. He finally agreed to meet with Mother Jones's delegation, though little was accomplished other than arousing public indignation about the mine operators and their increasingly brutal detectives, guards, and militiamen. Mother Jones had had serious dealings with corrupt, power-crazed militia before, notably in West Virginia coal mine strikes early in the twentieth century. She was moved to render a comparison: "I will give the military of West Virginia credit for one thing: they are far less brutal and cold blooded than the military of Colorado."[10]

The strike in southern Colorado was no longer simmering; it was heating to a boiling point as Christmas 1913 neared.

CHAPTER SEVENTEEN

A Different Christmas

IT'S FAIR TO SAY THAT MOTHER JONES was missing in action between the December 16 demonstration and the next account of her expulsion from the Trinidad coal field area on January 4. Where she spent Christmas is open to speculation.

What is known is how Christmas was celebrated in Ludlow. It was said to be a grim affair, marked by despair three months into the strike, with no end in sight. To lift their spirits, John Lawson, a major union leader, brought bags of candy and fruit for the strikers, who later feasted on rabbit stew or perhaps salami made from jackrabbits. There was little money for gifts, so mothers made rustic toys out of sticks and rocks, or ragdolls reworked from old clothes.

The nearby militia enjoyed a different sort of Christmas. Their mess hall in Trinidad was decorated with red and green lights and streamers. A band played sing-along Christmas music, and by the end of the evening, the officers were well fed on roast turkey and pumpkin pie.[1]

Sometime after the start of the new year, 1914, Mother Jones returned to the Trinidad area. General Chase again promised to arrest her if she did not leave the area. Undaunted, she shouted these words at a rally: "Tell General Chase that Mother Jones is going to Trinidad in a day or two and that he'd better play his strongest cards—the militia guns—against her. He had better go back to his mother and get a nursing bottle. He'll do better there than making war on an eighty-two year old woman."[2]

She and Chase were well-matched, two generals on the battlefield.

She headed back to Trinidad eight days later. But there were times when Mother Jones found jail inconvenient to her cause. In the past, when she had been banned from Trinidad, she sometimes snuck back in on a baggage car or cattle car, with the help of union railroad workers. This time, knowing that the militia would be watching for her at the Trinidad train station, she enlisted the aid of sympathetic railroad men who arranged for her train from Denver to lurch to an unscheduled stop, where she could get off. She walked the last few miles along the railroad tracks unnoticed and checked into the Toltec Hotel in Trinidad.

General Chase was furious when he discovered her ruse many hours later. His men burst into her hotel room and whisked her into an automobile. They took off as fast as the car would go with a "swarm of cavalrymen galloping behind the machine." The newspaper reported that Mother Jones was "loud in her denunciation of the military despots who stab and spit upon constitutional rights."[3]

Calling her a contentious witch, a rabble-rouser, and worse, General Chase jailed her in Mount San Rafael Hospital. That incarceration was what incited the demonstration that came to be called the Mother Jones Riot of January 21, 1914.

Though not charged with a crime, she was allowed no books or newspapers or visitors, except a lawyer and a doctor. She remained under heavy guard, and she described how "five big burly uniformed murderers with their guns on their shoulders and a belt of bullets around their stomachs and a saber hanging to their sides came up every night at six o'clock to put in twenty-four hours watching an old woman 82 years of age."[4]

Bored, eager for attention, and starved for company, Mother Jones played sick. Barron Beshoar wrote about a house call his father, Dr. Ben Beshoar, made to her. The guards would not let the doctor into her room, so he peered at her through the open door. She was sitting up in bed quite merrily. Dr. Beshoar, barely suppressing his laughter, called out, "Mother Jones! Mother Jones! Are you sick?"

She groaned loudly and faked a pitiful voice: "Oh, doctor, help me. I'm dying … I'm dying …"

The next day, newspapers around the country carried the cartoon of this absurd encounter, showing a poor old woman stretched out in a hospital bed and a brutal, unshaven soldier sticking his bayonet in Dr. Beshoar's stomach and crying, "Get out of here. No admission to you no matter how sick th' old woman is."

Dr. Beshoar's son called it "fine propaganda."[5] And propaganda, in its broadest sense, was the food that nourished Mary Harris Jones in her hunger to wrangle the spotlight and public support.

CHAPTER EIGHTEEN

High-Class Burglar

THE FAITHFUL WERE NOT WILLING to allow Mother Jones, their hero, to suffer in confinement without protest. On January 15, 1914, the mercury climbed to forty-eight degrees, making it the warmest January 15 in the history of Trinidad. Two hundred wives of strikers took advantage of the heat wave and swarmed the Columbian Hotel to confront General Chase. With babies and toddlers in tow, they belted out union songs and demanded that he release Mother Jones. He refused.[1]

Another day, nine hundred miners descended on Governor Ammons, threatening that if he didn't release Mother Jones, they'd storm San Rafael Hospital and do it themselves.[2] Again he refused, and the miners backed off.

Then on January 21, about a thousand women and children charged through the streets of Trinidad, singing, "the Union forever, hurrah! boys, hurrah!" and waving banners in the winter air proclaiming GOD BLESS MOTHER JONES!

The now well-known story is that the throng faced a line of cavalry with sabers unsheathed, and among them was General Chase. He is best remembered by union miners as the man who shouted, "Ride down the women!"

Women from Trinidad and the surrounding area marched in support of Mother Jones and the striking coal miners. The help and encouragement of the coal camp women was crucial to continuing the strike.

Mother Jones was suddenly released, without explanation, on March 16, after being held for nine weeks. Once again she was banished from the Trinidad area by General Chase and Governor Ammons, and sent to Denver. But she did not slink away quietly. Six days later, she was back, and General Chase locked her up again. This time, Chase was not to be made the fool. His troops boarded the train in Walsenburg, arrested her, and took her to the jail cell in the basement of Huerfano County Courthouse. The building had been condemned, but Chase deemed it good enough for the likes of Mother Jones.

In her autobiography, she said, "I was put in the cellar under the courthouse. It was a cold, terrible place, without heat, damp and dark. I slept in my clothes by day, and at night I fought great sewer rats with a beer bottle. 'If I were out of this dungeon,' I thought, 'I would be fighting the human sewer rats anyway!' "[3]

James Brewster, a University of Colorado professor, commented on her incarceration at the time: "The arrest of Mother Jones ... without a warrant, without any suspicion of crime, was one of the greatest outrages upon civilized American jurisprudence [justice].... Has it come to this that men so fear the truth that they must unlawfully imprison and silence this woman of eighty-two years?"[4]

Although she was kept incommunicado (meaning she wasn't allowed to see or speak to anyone on the outside), she managed, as usual, to get a letter smuggled out of the jail. She stuffed the letter in an empty beer bottle that had been rolling around under her cot. An unknown messenger carried the bottle down the river three miles, then released it to the public.[5]

"I ask the press to let the nation know of my treatment," Mother Jones wrote, "and to say to my friends ... that not even my incarceration in a damp underground dungeon will make me give up the fight in which I am engaged for liberty and for the rights of the working people. To be shut from the sunlight is not pleasant but ... I shall stand firm."[6]

She remained in the dark, rat-infested dungeon, with walls oozing putrid water, for twenty-six days. General Chase had no choice but to let her go, or face a losing court battle. She was freed on April 17, three days before the tragedy at Ludlow. In the sentiments of one biographer, "as un-American and criminal" as her confinement in Walsenburg was, it came to be a prelude to one of the "greatest catalysts of public opinion in the nation's history—the Ludlow Massacre."[7]

Once more, Chase told her never to show her face in Trinidad again, and this time she voluntarily left town. Sick and hobbled with arthritis pain from her confinement in the damp underground, she gathered the strength to go to Washington, D.C., to testify at a congressional hearing of the House Subcommittee on Mines and Mining. It was her dubious honor to speak after John D. Rockefeller Jr., major owner of CF&I.

Rockefeller made an incredible and noble statement, which was later etched on the exhibit tablets exhibited today at the Ludlow Monument. He said, "I believe that the prime consideration in the carrying on of an industry should be the well-being of the men and women engaged in it, and the soundest industrial policy which has constantly in mind the welfare of the employees as well as the making of profits, and which, when the necessity arises, subordinates profits to welfare." Rockefeller had never visited his properties in the canyons of Colorado, so he had no knowledge of how far this vision differed from the reality of the miners' lives and working conditions.

Typical of Mother Jones, her relationship with Rockefeller was both fascinating and contradictory. On the one hand, she called him a pirate, a hobo, a bum,[8] and a high-class burglar. In speech after speech, she named him the agent of misery for her beloved miners, and she sharply urged him to leave the sanctuary of his New York office and go west to see firsthand what the conditions were in the coal field.

On the other hand, the two rivals charmed one another, perhaps recognizing each other's extraordinary power. Mother Jones seemed convinced when Rockefeller swore that he was a changed man by the end of the strike. In fact, a year after the strike ended, she set her mud-dried

John D. Rockefeller on the left and his son, John D. Rockefeller Jr. John D. Rockefeller Jr. owned Colorado Fuel and Iron, the company that operated mines in southern Colorado. Mother Jones called him 'a high class burglar.'

boots down in Rockefeller's plush New York office and told him she no longer held him responsible for the conditions in the mines or the brutal actions of his mine guards.

At that time she assured him that she believed he never knew what "those hirelings out there were doing. I can see how easy it is to misguide you," she said.[9]

For his part, offering a handshake in front of a press eager for a rich photo opportunity, Rockefeller teased her about throwing compliments his way after all the treacherous words that she had rained upon him previously.

Mother Jones laughed and responded in her characteristically witty manner, "Yes, I am more inclined to throw bricks."[10]

CHAPTER NINETEEN

Four Feet of Feathers

"I HAVE LEARNED THAT MEN are as big mouthed as women and are just as empty brained," Mother Jones said.[1] Not a flattering picture of women or men! Her scorn for men was usually reserved for those who didn't have the courage to join a union or fight for their rights.

Just in case women smugly thought they were blameless, she also said, "How a woman can degrade herself by marrying a measly man who does not dare to join a union is beyond my comprehension."[2]

A case could be made for the fact that Mother Jones didn't much like human beings in general, except in the abstract as laborers and soldiers in the working-class battle. She once said that she didn't believe in women's rights or men's rights, only in human rights.[3]

However, for women, her scorn was limitless. Mother Jones had an intense dislike for women, but she put up with them and could even be civil to them, if they contributed to the welfare of "the grimy-faced sons of labor."[4] Otherwise, she labeled women frivolous, vain, gossipy, naïve, materialistic, idle, faddish, extravagant, and overly sentimental beings who filled their heads with nonsense such as suffrage and **Prohibition**.[5]

Her most scathing comments were lavished upon rich women. With no lack of her own ego strength, she contrasted them with women such as herself: "A lady is a female whose skull is adorned with four feet of feathers. A woman is one whose skull is full of gray matter—studying the conditions beneath the surface." She continued, "It nauseates me to see your average city woman. She is always overdressed, although she is careful to leave her right hand bared so that she can display her fingers crowded to their utmost with jewels."[6]

Mother Jones had little use for women involved in charity work (which she called a fad) or in women's right to vote. Such work, though well-meaning, drew energy away from what Mother Jones considered the *real* issues: class war and workers' struggles. She believed that women corrupted an election because they could be bought for a "pair of nice gloves."[7] The average woman was unfit for the ballot, she proclaimed, offering Colorado as a prime example of the ineffectiveness of women voting. In Colorado, women had been allowed to run for office since the mid-1890s, but what good had that done them, when working men and women, especially miners, were still in slavery?[8]

In 1914 Mother Jones was the guest of honor at a dinner attended by five hundred women writers, artists, philanthropists, and suffragists. A more gracious keynote speaker would have made generous remarks. Mother Jones, however, railed against woman suffrage, saying, "I have no vote, and I've raised hell all over the country!" The audience was shocked.[9]

In an interview in the *New York Times*, she said, "In no sense of the word am I in sympathy with woman's suffrage. ... women are out of place in political work."[10] Where should they be? At home, she said, caring for and educating children, keeping their husbands out of the saloons and pool halls, and fighting beside the men for workers' rights. In fact, she went so far as to accuse women of neglecting motherhood in their vain effort to enter the political arena, and claimed that this neglect had kept the juvenile courts busy and filled reform schools.[11]

Mother Jones was not the only one who thought that elaborate women's hats were frivolous and silly. This cartoon seems to make the point that voting rights for women were as silly as overly decorated hats.

The cartoon's caption reads, "When women vote. What will happen if the polling place is located in a millinery shop?" implying that women would buy hats and forget to vote.

Such criticism of women goes a long way to explain why she had few female friends but many radical admirers and a battalion of working-class women worshippers. Bottle washers in the Wisconsin breweries and textile mill laborers relied on her to help them wage their battles. But it was with the miners' wives that she had the most sway. She assured Colorado miners that the key to a successful strike was their wives.

"Every woman should arise," Mother Jones implored, to stand "side by side with her brother, working on the battlefield, urging him to keep on in this desperate struggle until victory is ours."[12]

Women seized upon her call. In January 1914, they formed the United Women of the Mine Workers and applied to the Colorado Federation of Labor for a charter. It may have had as many as 500 members, but it did not survive long.[13] However, a grassroots group took action and did battle with whatever weapons they had in their kitchens and front yards. The "mop and broom" brigade showed up first in West Virginia and then in Colorado, with women ferociously banging pots and pans in their protests.

They were a mighty force, these women.

CHAPTER TWENTY

Tinwillies and Fierce Warriors

SCABS! A WHOLE TRAINLOAD! ARRIVING THIS MORNING! Word of replacement workers spread like prairie fire through Ludlow Tent Colony in November 1913, two months into the strike.

While the men were out of work, the women did not stand by helplessly. They turned their frustration and rage on the strikebreakers and made weapons of brooms, mops, buckets, and skillets. Wielding these along with clubs, baseball bats, hammers, billiard cues, and tree limbs, some studded with nails or sharpened to lethal points, the women waited at the Ludlow train depot to head off the expected throng of strikebreakers. If the scabs managed to get past the women and to the mines, a second group of women and children waited at the mine entrance, beating pans with hammers to unnerve the mine guards. Neither the guards nor the scabs were willing to remove the women and children physically. Often the strikebreakers simply left or, desperate for work, retreated and hoped to outwait and outwit the women and get into the mines later.

To the women's disappointment, sometimes rumors of the arrival of scabs proved false, and the women returned to their tents, primed for the next battle.[1] As Mother Jones was fond of saying, "An army of strong mining women makes a wonderfully spectacular picture."[2]

A decade later, a prominent Illinois union activist named Agnes Wieck described how an army of Mother Jones's women stood behind the striking men "like a wall of steel that nothing could batter down." Mother Jones inspired coal miners' wives and mothers to take heart when daily life grew more challenging as the strike dragged on through the winter months. Wieck wrote that Mother Jones's words "gave voice to such women; her speeches helped them make sense of their experience, brought shape and poetry and meaning to their lives."[3]

Ironically, violence came with that poetry and meaning. At the Walsen mine, women and children massed at the main gate when scabs were quitting for the day. They used everything within their means to persuade these men to join the union and not to return to the mines the next day. But soon gentle persuasion escalated into an ugly scene. One strikebreaker, John Hale, refused to join the union and apparently got surly with the women. They chased him, knocked him down, rolled him in the mud, and kicked him. Mine guards rushed to his rescue, and most of the women scuttled away, but one refused to give up the fight. She jumped on Hale and beat him over the head with a heavy bucket, breaking his nose and cutting his face.[4]

Occasionally women raised their sticks and clubs against other mining women whose husbands had returned to work out of desperation.[5] More commonly, though, women maintained a peaceful protest, night and day, to prevent strikebreakers from entering the mines. Singing union songs and often holding their babies on their shoulders, they formed a picket line, a human barricade that the scabs would have to break through to get to work. They'd create such a "rumpus" (Mother Jones's homespun word) with their howling and clanging pans that even the mules were spooked and refused to do their jobs.

Fulfilling Mother Jones's proclamation that the destiny of this nation lies in its women,[6] mining wives also trained their children to be small soldiers in the coal field war. Children were especially skillful at taunting the militiamen, calling them "scab herders" and "tinwillies."[7] *Tinwillies* was a common insult of the time and implied that the men weren't real, respectable, courageous soldiers.

Examples abound of tough, fearless women smuggling guns and ammunition to the miners in the bullpens. Angela Tonso, a **Tyrolean** resident of Ludlow, reported in her broken English, "We put the rifle under our coat there, and half in the boots and half under the arm, and have our arm free so the militia they see that we ain't got nothing."[8]

How effective were these women? Quite effective. This was a time in our history, at the end of the Victorian era, when women were considered the weaker sex and models of virtue. Behind the shield of their modest femininity, miners' wives courageously rebelled in ways for which their husbands would have been beaten or thrown into the bullpen or banished from future work in the mines. The mine guards, hired detectives who were little more than thugs, and militiamen were reluctant to lay a hand on these women. So the women enjoyed a certain immunity from violence and punishment. In fact, they seized the beginnings of change in gender roles, allowing females to become powerful activists. They followed the dual example

Mother Jones had set: sacred, untouchable mother and, at the same time, fierce warrior.[9]

Delivering her customary mixed message, Mother Jones inspired their activism, even violent actions, but also laid the heavy armor of responsibility on their shoulders. She preached that their main responsibilities were to their husbands, children, and home. Keep the men out of the saloons and don't let them go back to work until they get their demands met. Educate the children and give them moral grounding. Scrimp and make do with whatever little there is; take in boarders or laundry if necessary. Above all, keep the home stable for the men so they can carry on the union's goals. The message Mother Jones delivered, as interpreted by Zeese Papanikolas, was this:

> "It is not the demonstration or violence or the speeches that will win this strike, if it is won, but the simple continuity of feeding and washing and cleaning that goes on between those canvas walls, those trips along the muddy paths between the wash lines and the coal piles and the store. And if the women give up one day on the scrimping and hoarding and patching and say they've had enough, then the strike is lost."[10]

Mother Jones was not the only female organizing women during the strike, though she may have been the most visible and outspoken. A moderate group called the Women's Peace Association operated in southern Colorado through the political process rather than in the trenches of the coal camps. Led by Anna Steele, widow of a former chief justice of the Colorado Supreme Court, this group was a colorful hodge-podge of middle-class women of leisure in beautiful hats and furs, and working-class women in calico dresses with babies blanketed in their arms. Among them was Helen Ring Robinson, a Colorado state senator. The group's mission was not to take sides—they

The wives and children of the striking miners were staunch supporters of the men. Mother Jones encouraged them to help the men continue the strike. Sometimes, they joined the battle by fighting scabs and mine guards.

EARLY TWENTIETH-CENTURY WOMEN IN THE LABOR MOVEMENT

Mother Jones wasn't the only woman involved in the early twentieth-century labor movement, although she liked to believe that she was the only one who counted.

- The **Women's Trade Union League** (WTUL) formed in 1903 to aid working women. Its membership embraced women of the upper, middle, and lower classes. The WTUL shed light on the working conditions of women, organized them into unions, and took part in labor disputes, especially during the garment workers' strikes between 1909 and 1913. The WTUL was a link between the woman suffrage campaigns, dominated by wealthy women, and the issues confronting working-class women. Mother Jones was not a fan of the WTUL because of its inclusion of women she called "clubgoers and lazy shirkers." She didn't actively oppose their efforts; she merely ignored them in her speeches and letters. (For more on the WTUL, see Sheila Rawbotham's *A Century of Women: The History of Women in Britain and the United States*. New York: Viking, 1977.)

- **Mollie Schepps**, a shirtwaist factory worker and suffragist. She famously said "Equal say will enable women to get equal pay."

- **Elizabeth Gurley Flynn**, an outspoken opponent of Schepps. More akin to Mother Jones's views, Flynn's point was that economic change in the workplace, not the vote, was the key to improving the lot of working women.

- **Mary Macarthur**, a British suffragist, said, "Knowledge is power. Organization is power. Knowledge and organization mean the opening of the cage door."

- **Clara Lemlich**, a Jewish union activist and leader of the 1909 strike by the International Ladies' Garment Workers' Union against New York textile manufacturers. She spoke to huge crowds of immigrants like herself in their native tongue, Yiddish, urging them to strike for better wages and working conditions.

were not for the strikers or the mine operators—but to appeal to Governor Ammons "to take steps to bring this civil war to an end." They didn't belt out labor songs like "the union forever, hurrah, boys, hurrah!" They quietly and forcefully sang "America" and "The Battle Hymn of the Republic" in the capitol rotunda in Denver. They swore to stay in the building until the governor would meet with them, which he did, briefly.[11]

It would surprise no one that Mother Jones was not an enthusiastic fan of this group or of the Women's Trade Union League, which supported working women in their quest for better conditions. She zealously guarded the limelight and was unwilling to share it with other women, especially those she considered the sentimental "parlor parasites." But she didn't oppose either organization as forcefully as she did the suffragists. She merely ignored them, rendering them irrelevant.

Here's one last example of Mother Jones's mixed feelings about women. We know she held women in contempt unless they were poor, working class, staunch warriors in the union battles. We know she was shamelessly blunt about the futility of women voting and seeking office. Nevertheless, she made a startling comment about President Theodore Roosevelt's lack of compassion during her 1903 march in support of the mill children. "You fellows do elect wonderful presidents," she said in an interview. "The best thing you can do is to put a woman in the next time."[12]

CHAPTER TWENTY-ONE

A Great Principle

LUDLOW WAS UNDER MILITARY OCCUPATION, or maybe it wasn't. No one knew for sure. But General Chase was acting as though Governor Ammons had declared **martial law** in the tent colony. The governor had directed Chase to use his best "judgment and discretion."[1] Some would say that the general's judgment was questionable, and he appeared to have little discretion. Gunfire continued to thunder over the colony. The miners were prepared to defend their territory. The situation was potentially explosive and attracted attention in Washington.

In February 1914, while Mother Jones was still imprisoned in Walsenburg, the U.S. Congress began an investigation. Five delegates from the Foster Committee, the House Subcommittee on Mines and Mining, traveled to Denver to take testimony from people on both sides of the dispute.

When the Denver interviews were done, the congressmen moved on to Trinidad to talk to more witnesses. Finally, they braved the punishing winter on the prairie and visited Ludlow itself. Citizens in the tent colony greeted them with a brass band and wild cheers, just as they had greeted the Colorado National Guard months earlier.

The congressmen passed out candy and nickels to the children as they walked through the colony. Their observations of the harsh life in Ludlow—the flimsy tents, the outdoor latrines, the trash piles, the culm banks, the hungry children—would surely touch their hearts. Ludlow's adults believed that the committee's visit would make their plight public, and public opinion would force the mine owners to compromise on the strikers' demands for better pay and safer working conditions.[2]

General Chase refused to testify before the Foster Committee, but the guns were silent for the duration of the investigation.

In April, Mother Jones was released from her Walsenburg dungeon jail and traveled to Washington to testify before the Foster Committee. Her testimony wasn't always coherent, dotted with her usual folksy tales, exaggerations, and convenient memories. She was very clear, however, when she stated her belief that the coal mines should be under national control, and that President Wilson ought to be sending federal troops to the coal fields.

Just before her testimony, CF&I's owner, John D. Rockefeller Jr., appeared before the same congressional hearing. He was the multimillionaire about whom Mother Jones said, "'Tis an outrage indeed that Rockefeller should own the coal that God put in the earth for all people."[3]

On April 5, 1914, with Mother Jones in the front row listening, the coal company owner defended the idea of an open shop, meaning one that is not unionized. Despite the strikers' detailed list of demands, Rockefeller claimed that the miners had no dissatisfaction with their working conditions. He'd distributed pamphlets describing how "perfectly happy was the life of the miner until the agitators came." Mother Jones was proud to be the most notorious and thorny agitator.

Congressman Martin Foster of Illinois was the chairman of the House Subcommittee on Mines and Mining, before which Rockefeller testified. Foster seemed stunned that Rockefeller had not visited the turbulent coal field during those first seven months of the strike, which was now becoming a minor civil war. Foster challenged Rockefeller with more of an accusation than a question: "You are willing to let these killings take place rather than to go there and do something to settle conditions?"

With stoic composure, Rockefeller offered this startling response, "There is just one thing that can be done to settle this strike, and that is to unionize the camps, and our interest in labor is so profound and we believe so sincerely that that interest demands that the camps shall be open camps, that we expect to stand by the officers at any cost."

Congressman Foster replied, "And you will do that if it costs all your property and kills all your employees?"

Rockefeller replied, "It is a great principle."[4]

That principle was tested during the desperate days in mid-April 1914.

Despite more than two months of testimony from various people involved in the coal field war, the only noticeable change was that Governor Ammons withdrew about eighty percent of state troops from the war zone. That decision had less to do with the congressional investigation and more to do with the financial drain on the state. The troops' departure left about two hundred soldiers of various stripes, ranging from CF&I mine guards and pit bosses to professional soldiers, to hired "detectives" who actually functioned as enforcers.[5] Most were encamped at Cedar Hill, two miles from Ludlow. Twenty or so militiamen remained poorly sheltered in three tents on Water Tank Hill, in clear sight of approximately four hundred Ludlow union men. Each side had guns aimed at the other. Chase's troops expected a massive attack by the striking men. They believed the strikers would shoot to kill and then take control of all the mines and throw out the scabs Chase was supposed to protect.

Sunday, April 19, was Easter, according to the Greek Orthodox calendar.* At Ludlow Tent Colony, it was a day of mixed blessings. The atmosphere was both celebratory and tense. Residents sang this version of the "Battle Hymn of the Republic" during the holiday festivities:

> There's a fight in Colorado for to set the miners free,
> From the tyrants and the money-kings and all the powers that be;
> They have trampled on the freedom that was meant for you and me,
> But Right is marching on.
> Cheer, boys, cheer the cause of union
> The Colorado Miners Union
> Glory, glory to our Union,
> Our cause is marching on. [6]

Despite the simmering restlessness, the community enjoyed a feast of rabbit stew and ethnic dishes the women created from their meager stores of food and early spring gardens. There was dancing and multi-national music played on violins and accordions and guitars.[7] And of

*The Western Christian Church establishes the movable date of Easter according to the Gregorian calendar. The Eastern Orthodox Church, however, uses the older Julian calendar. To further complicate matters, the Orthodox Easter cannot occur before the Jewish Passover. Thus, Western Easter was celebrated at Ludlow on April 12, 1914—a full week before Orthodox Easter and eight days before the Ludlow tragedy.

course, a baseball game. The married and single men and boys played against wives, mothers, and sisters decked out in bloomers.

As often happened, a few of the soldiers came to watch the game, but that day they brought their rifles with them. According to a later report from Pearl Jolly, the camp nurse, four soldiers walked right on the field, swearing and yelling with their rifles raised, trying to intimidate the base runners. One of the Ludlow women laughed and teased a soldier who'd strolled right into the middle of the diamond. He responded, "That's right, girlie, you have your big Sunday today and tomorrow we will have the roast."[8]

Maybe he was just posturing and boasting in the face of ridicule from a woman. Or maybe he was revealing the militia's plan that the entire colony would go up in smoke before the next day's sunset.

When the baseball games and singing and holiday feasting were over, and the militiamen had gone to their tents on Water Tank Hill, the Ludlow residents went to bed, jittery about what the next morning would bring. Watchmen stood guard over the colony all through the night.

Mother Jones once promised miners, "I will be with you at midnight or when the battle rages, when the last bullet ceases."[9] But she was not there when Ludlow erupted the next morning.

CHAPTER TWENTY-TWO

Warlike Spirit

JUST BEFORE SUNRISE ON APRIL 20, Ludlow watchmen anxiously eyed Water Tank Hill, where soldiers pointed their machine guns at the tent colony. Water Tank Hill was optimistically named, in the same way a French poodle might be called Brutus, for the hill, three-quarters of a mile away from the tent colony, was actually a small mesa rising only slightly over the flat prairie. The position gave the dozen soldiers encamped there a good view of the tent colony and a clear aim.

No one knows who fired the first shots. Each side accused the other of firing first.[1] In truth, the militiamen and Ludlow's red-bandana men had been firing shots at each other for months. As early as October 7, two weeks after the strike was called, a pitched gun battle had taken place. That morning, though, something felt more threatening than the usual indifferent spray of gunfire. Watchmen began running through the colony waking everyone, urging them to seek shelter.

On Water Tank Hill, militiamen prepared three crude bombs that were not designed to cause a great deal of damage. They hurled the bombs into the tent colony, possibly as a warning to cease firing. Ludlow men interpreted this action as a deliberate attack and were inflamed with a "warlike spirit."[2] Bullets flew toward the soldiers on the hill. All the men stood on alert. Sporadic gunfire continued from both sides.

"Look out! The militia is coming!" someone shouted, whether or not it was true.

Mary Thomas cried, "I think there's going to be trouble." She urged her neighbors to grab their children and run as fast as they could to hide. With one daughter in her arms and another hanging on her skirt, Mary herded several other children to any safe place they could find as gunfire sprayed over the tents.[3] Women grabbed their young ones and dashed to the small pump house across the railroad tracks, or into the nearly dry **arroyo** (wide ditch), just yards north of the tent colony.

From their position on Water Tank Hill, the Colorado National Guard could fire at will on the Ludlow Tent Colony below.

"The prairie was covered with human beings running in all directions like ants … not even thinking through the clouds of panic," Mary Thomas said later.[4] Bullets rocketed over their heads. Mary Thomas suffered a minor gunshot wound to her wrist (or, by other accounts, to her foot). A neighbor bound up the wound with a bandage torn from her own petticoat, and Mary hurried on with the children clinging to her. Eight women and fifteen children scurried down into the arroyo as they heard a blast from one of the small bombs fired from Water Tank Hill.

Frank Snyder, his parents, and his five brothers and sisters huddled in the damp dugout under the floorboards of their tent, dodging the gunfire that showered over the colony. Their position below ground mercifully muffled the sounds blaring through the colony. These fortified pits had been dug shortly after Ludlow colony had been established, to expand living space and storage space, and to provide shelter from the harsh winter and summer extremes. But on April 20, they became shelters from gunfire.

When Alcarita Pedregone spotted the militiamen on Water Tank Hill early that morning, she quickly lifted the floorboards beneath her bed and hustled her two young children down into the pit. In a short time, Mrs. Costa and Mrs. Valdez and their six children joined the Pedregones. Eleven of them crowded together for the entire day, with little air to breathe and no way to stand and stretch their legs.

Mary Petrucci and her children took refuge in the dugout beneath their own tent, as did James Fyler, the colony's paymaster and his family. Other women and children made the frantic dash between bullets and clambered down ladders into a large railroad water well between the colony and the arroyo. As one of them said, they might as well drown as be shot.[5] The well was fairly dry, except at the very bottom, and it was twenty feet across, good and large. But by the end of the day, there were seventy mothers and children tottering on unstable platforms over the water or actually standing in putrid, stagnant water.

A girl of seven named Helen Korich was urged to flee to the well, but she was immobilized by fear and clung to her father, who needed to stay behind to fight the battle. Helen later described the scene this way: "The shells were flying all around our heads. I wanted to go with my father. We were out of the tent, and I wouldn't let him go.... My mother had to send my sister out to get me, and she pulled me by the hair until I let go of him. I was so mad! I knew my dad was going to get killed."[6]

The man in charge of the pump house, who lived in a refurbished boxcar, provided what little food and drink he could spare for the people in hiding. Mary Thomas risked her own safety to dash between the pump house, the well, and the arroyo to deliver more food and water.

With the chaos of gunfire all around them, the strikers struggled to keep their rifles loaded. Mary had never handled a gun before, but one of the men quickly showed her how to reload the barrels. The battle raged on.

Helen Korich, her two sisters, and her mother, who was clutching their baby brother, all rushed to the well, staying inches ahead of the bullets. Helen later reported that the family dog and her puppy ran with them toward the well. Helen said, "They shot her. ... They killed the puppy, too. ... I remember how quiet everything was ... You could hear all the shooting, buy nobody yelled. ... They were going to kill us all."[7]

CHAPTER TWENTY-THREE

Louis Tikas

PEARL JOLLY RAN FROM TENT TO TENT to warn and comfort people and treat minor wounds. During the chaos of that day, Louis Tikas rose to his highest level of leadership, directing the men on the firing line and making sure the women and children were relatively safe in hiding places.

Husbands and fathers fell to bullets before their horrified families. One bullet shattered the skull of a man named Frank Rubio as he led several women and children to the arroyo.

Both sides sent for reinforcements, and men poured in to take part in this bloody skirmish. A doctor from out of town, Aca Harvey, hurried to the site to tend to the wounded strikers. Seeing that bullets were flying, Dr. Harvey waved a white flag to show that he wasn't a combatant and later reported, "Every time I stuck it out, it would be shot at."[1]

Was there no one among them to stop this insane aggression? One man, Louis Tikas, attempted to diffuse some of the violent energy on that April morning. Tikas put his life on the line and agreed to meet with an enemy commander, Major Pat Hamrock, in neutral territory at the railroad tracks about halfway between Ludlow and Water Tank Hill.

Louis Tikas

Before the meeting, Hamrock phoned his men two miles away on Cedar Hill, requesting backup, and he issued this order: "Put that baby in the buggy and bring it along with you."[5] Decoded, this meant bring the machine gun to the meeting with Tikas.

That tense meeting took place about nine o'clock that morning, and the two men appeared to settle their differences and agreed to stop shooting. On his way back to the colony, Tikas observed that the redneck strikers had stealthily advanced on the militia and were hiding in an arroyo. He waved a white handkerchief, the universal signal of peace, to urge the Ludlow men to hold fire and return to their tents. This signal was also meant for the militia on the hill.

Tikas's white flag was ignored by both sides. The random gunfire grew into an intense battle of crossfire that continued through the day.

Tikas spent most of that harrowing day with Pearl Jolly. The two of them were trying to calm Ludlow residents who were near panic.[6] From here, the events become part speculation because the full story isn't known. Sometime around dusk, Tikas decided to surrender himself in exchange for a truce. Or maybe that's not the way it happened at all. Louis Tikas became something of a legend, and legends by definition are more exaggeration than fact. What is known of this dramatic incident comes not from his comrades but from the militia. By their account, Tikas was running from the flaming tents when soldiers captured him as their trophy of war.[7]

As well as the jigsaw can be pieced together, this may be how Louis Tikas spent his last moments:

A cry goes out: "We've got Louie the Greek!" Colorado National Guardsmen surround him, along with a ragtag crowd of volunteer militia. They're cursing and shouting at him. Some call for a rope to hang him. They've also captured James Fyler, and another man whose name has been lost to history.

Lieutenant Karl Linderfelt, not known for his compassion, confronts Tikas. "I thought you were going to stop this," he says, meaning the violence, the bloodshed, the burning tents. The two men exchange angry words and accusations. Tikas calls Linderfelt a name "any man with red blood in his veins will not stand." The lieutenant raises the butt of his Springfield rifle and swings it onto Tikas's head with such force that the rifle breaks in two. The blow leaves a wound deep enough to show bone.

As in the accounts of the Mother Jones Riot, there are at least two versions of what happens next. In one, Tikas miraculously remains standing despite the gaping wound spurting blood. In another version, he collapses facedown in his own blood, and Linderfelt stomps away in disgust, promising that Tikas will not be lynched, despite cries to hang him, hang

Louis the Greek. Linderfelt washes his hands of the matter, muttering, "I broke or spoiled an awful good rifle."[8]

The end result, however, was the same in all versions. Tikas lay dead.

The official report from the militia was that Louis Tikas and James Fyler were accidently killed in crossfire. A coroner's inquest revealed that Tikas had actually been shot in the back three times at close range.

Godfrey Irwin, a man who happened to be traveling in southern Colorado at the time, claimed to have seen Tikas's final moments, and his account was closer to the coroner's than to the militia's. After the blow from Linderfelt's rifle butt, Irwin said, "Tikas fell face downward. As he lay there we saw the militiamen fall back. Then they aimed their rifles and deliberately fired them into the unconscious man's body. It was the first murder I had ever seen, for it was a murder and nothing less."[9] Irwin's report may have been long on drama but short on accuracy, since he never mentioned the lesser known James Fyler who was with Tikas and whose body, like Tikas's, lay by the railroad tracks for hours before they were taken home.

Also short on fact are the scandalous recollections of Mary Hannah Thomas O'Neal, sixty years later. She recalled that Pearl was an incurable flirt who went so far as to flirt with the enemy militia men. Mary claimed that the soldiers were jealous of Tikas's relationship with Pearl Jolly, and that is why they killed him.[10]

Nothing supports this allegation. It's not unlike another rumor designed to discredit Mother Jones. A Denver newspaper reporter named Polly Pry wrote that Mother Jones was running from a shady past. Both of these stories are highly unlikely, and so they smolder together in the fascinating realm of rumor.

Meanwhile, the battle raged on in Ludlow.

CHAPTER TWENTY-FOUR

The Thirteen

MAYBE MARY PETRUCCI YEARNED for the comfort of her neighbors rather than staying alone with her children in the pit under her own tent, which was aflame and turning to ash. Toward evening, she hauled her children to the surface. They dashed to a nearby tent and squeezed down into a dugout with the Pedregones, the Costas, and the Valdezes. Mrs. Petrucci left the entrance hole uncovered to capture a bit of a breeze from above, and even still, there was precious little air to breath. Fifteen people were jammed together in a dugout about eight feet long, six feet high, and four-and-a-half feet wide. All of them gasped for mouthfuls of cool, clean air as tents burned all around the colony.

Suddenly, the tent above these four underground families began to burn, as well. Smoke wafted down into the dugout. The mothers and children were too cramped together to climb out. One by one they were overcome by smoke. Then the unimaginable happened—the bed in the tent above their pit collapsed in the fire, and its charred remains covered the hole. With no oxygen coming in, the women and children all fell unconscious.

Dusk settled in, and the guns grew curiously still. Frank Snyder raised the planks that covered the pit under his family's tent and hoisted himself out of the hole. His brother George followed.

Here, again, the stories take different paths. The most colorfully told are in the books by Scott Martelle and Zeese Papanikolas, from which we surmise the events:

Frank and George see no one, hear no whirshing of bullets. Frank steals into the clearing between two tents, in search of water for his thirsty family below ground.

How could he know that the militia is under orders to shoot anything that moves, even a dog, even chickens? He's glad to stretch his gangly legs, and so he becomes an easy target.

A shot rips across the clearing. George cries out, "Frank's been shot!"

William Snyder hears the gunshot and George's cry. He climbs to the surface and rushes to his son. Frank Snyder, just days away from his twelfth birthday, lies dead, the back of his head blown away.

The father lifts his boy and yells down into the pit, "Frank is dead!"

Mrs. Snyder climbs to the surface, swoons at the sight of her firstborn, as her husband tries to clean the boy's face of the blood.

A militia soldier steps near the family, ignores the shattered body, and yanks Mrs. Snyder and her daughter up, cursing at the family and ordering them to get out, run.

Shocked, Mr. Snyder asks the soldier to help him carry the boy, but the soldier responds, "Aren't you big enough to do it yourself?" He grabs the boy's body and throws it on the ground outside the tent. "Here, carry the damn thing yourself," he shouts.[1]

The family is stunned with grief, and doesn't yet know that Tikas is dead. William feels he must tell Tikas that they've lost

Frank. He stumbles out of the tent. The militia's machine gun spots him and chases him with its rat-a-tat-tat, almost as sport.

In William Snyder's own words:

"I got back home and I got down on the floor and took both of Frank's hands—he was just drawing up—and laid them across his chest."[2] *He prepares to carry Frank down into the pit when other militiamen burst into the tent. They soak the canvas with kerosene and set it on fire.*

Was the tent set ablaze deliberately, or, as later reports suggested, did the Snyder tent and others ignite when bullets stored in the tents exploded? The final report by Dr. Jaffe, the county coroner, affirmed that the "fire on tents was started by militiamen under Major Hamrock and Lieutenant Linderfelt, or mine guards, or both."[3] What actually happened remains uncertain. What *is* certain, graphically reported by eyewitnesses, is that within a short time, dozens of tents were ablaze throughout the colony.

Godfrey Irwin, that same traveler who witnessed Louis Tikas's death, also claims to have seen the tent burnings. "We watched from our rock shelter while the militia dragged up their machine guns and poured a murderous fire into the arroyo from a height by Water Tank Hill above the Ludlow depot. Then came the firing of the tents. I am positive that by no possible chance could they have been set ablaze accidentally."[4]

Irwin's account is suspect, however, as there are no reports of fire in the arroyo, where so many women and children had fled. More believable is the report of Mrs. Donner, a Ludlow resident, who witnessed "invading troops use flaming brooms dipped in coal oil to ignite tents."[5]

The most persuasive evidence came from a militia officer: "[M]en and soldiers swarmed into the colony and deliberately assisted the **conflagration** by spreading the fire from tent to tent ... beyond a doubt, it was seen to, intentionally, that the fire should destroy the whole of the colony."[6]

In fact, it did, but not before soldiers stole whatever they could carry away—pots and pans, beds, a sewing machine.

Still stunned with shock and sorrow, the Snyder family wends its way between burning tents and gunfire to the Ludlow train depot half a mile south. William carries their three-year-old daughter in one arm and Frank's body over his shoulder. They encounter Lieutenant Karl Linderfelt, who had stood by when Tikas and Fyler were shot in the back. Linderfelt shines his flashlight in William's face and curses the grief-stricken father.[7]

Eventually the Snyders reach the depot and encamp on the floor, with Frank's body wrapped in a sheet, or according to another account, a gunny sack. They wait all night for the train to Trinidad, jeered by militia men who are boasting about their accomplishments of the day and serenading one another with an accordion and a violin looted from the Ludlow tents.[8]

Still underground in their stifling pit and surrounded by lifeless bodies, Mary Petrucci and Alcarita Pedregone miraculously recovered consciousness. They tried to rouse their children and the other two mothers, but it was no use. Mrs. Petrucci and Mrs. Pedregone clawed and scrabbled their way to the hot surface for air and help.

They succeeded, but none of their children survived.

CHAPTER TWENTY-FIVE

Remember Ludlow!

THE BATTLE RAGED ON FOR FOURTEEN HOURS. The mild April day yielded to a biting night chill, with women and children huddling in the well and the arroyo. They could see the smoke of the smoldering tents. All were hungry and thirsty, and mothers had nothing to give their children, not even assurance. Mary Thomas was able to deliver small amounts of food and water to them, at great risk to herself. She urgently warned the women that they couldn't stay in their hiding places, because as soon as the soldiers were through looting the burnt tents, they'd come looking for escapees.

A sympathetic rancher named Frank Bayes was willing to give them shelter. The problem was that the ranch was on open prairie. As soon as the women and children crawled out of hiding, they would become targets for the soldiers.

Many of their lives were saved because of a train. The women knew when a freight train was due to pass by. They waited patiently for the long train to approach the Ludlow depot. As soon as it blocked the view between the arroyo and Water Tank Hill, the women shoved and carried their children up the ladders or up the sides of the arroyo. They ran as fast as possible toward the ranch, two miles away. The Bayes family took them in and fed them. Many made beds on the floor of the stable, warmed and covered by hay.

While their children fell into a deep sleep, some of the mothers spent a good part of the night on their knees. They were of various Christian denominations, but that night they all prayed fervently for the same things: for their lives, the lives of their husbands still in harm's way, and a home to return to.

By the time darkness blanketed the smoldering colony, countless people were injured, many were dead, and all were homeless.

The number of fatalities varied in different reports. The United Mine Workers *Journal* reported that thirty-three men, women, and children lay dead. A more realistic number appeared in the April 21 *Trinidad Chronicle-News*[1] where a headline screamed:

25 Dead, 3 Wounded

TENT COLONY SWEPT OUT OF EXISTENCE

An article on the current UMW website states that twenty people lost their lives that tragic day. Seven perished by gunfire, including three unnamed militiamen, one innocent bystander, Louis Tikas, James Fyler, and Frank Snyder.

The remaining fatalities were the two women and eleven children who suffocated in the pit beneath a burning tent.

Their names are to be preserved. These mothers and children perished together: Fedelina (Cedi) Costa and her two children, Onofrio and Lucy, ages six and four; Patria Valdez and her four children, Rudolph, Eulala, Mary, and

Elvira, ages nine, eight, seven, and three months. Then there are the children of the two surviving mothers, Mary Petrucci and Alcarita Pedregone, who had miraculously escaped the smothering tomb: Joe, Lucy, and Frank Petrucci, ages four, three, and six months; and Rodgerio and Cloriva Pedregone, ages nine and four.

Two mothers, nine children, nine and under, plus two infants yet to see their first birthday.

Each life is vitally important, but the accurate number of fatalities is less so. What's key here is that the term *massacre* that came to be associated with this event, referred mostly to the women and children who had smothered in the dark pit below ground.

There are two sad ironies associated with the deaths in the pit. The first is its size. It was larger than most of the community's underground shelters, suggesting that it was used as a maternity ward for the colony. A place where babies had come into life became a death trap for children. The second irony is that the men had struck against the mine operators to change the inhumane conditions in mines deep beneath the surface—and now, thirteen of their loved ones had perished below ground.

An editorial writer for the *Rocky Mountain News* summed up the entire tragedy this way: "The horror of the shambles at Ludlow is overwhelming.... The blood of the women and children, burned and shot like rats, cries aloud from the ground. The great state of Colorado has failed them."[2]

By morning, the militia was gone. The striking fighters came out of the hills, and either rode to Trinidad in a union truck or straggled back to Ludlow. Once there, they found their colony in utter ruin, smoke still billowing and the ashes still warm. Twisted bed frames. Cast-iron stoves with food still in the ovens. Piles of half-burned clothes and bedding. Shards of glass and pottery. Toys and pots and pans and washtubs riddled with bullets. An unnamed telephone lineman sifting through the ruins lifted a twisted iron cot and discovered what has been called "the black hole of Ludlow"— the pit with the bodies of the thirteen who had suffocated.[3]

A truce was called at least until all the militia casualties and Ludlow dead could be laid to rest. Mother Jones heard of the destruction of Ludlow while she was in Washington, D.C., urging Congress and President Wilson to intervene in the coal field war. She hurried back to Ludlow in time for the funerals. In an attempt to bolster the morale of grieving miners and their families, she said, "Here I am again, boys, just back from Washington, and you aren't licked by a whole lot.... Washington is aroused and there is help coming.... Go home, boys. Mind me now and keep cool."[4]

Ludlow Tent Colony as it looked on April 29, 1914, two weeks after the Ludlow Massacre.

They "boys" of Ludlow took her advice, but not so the enraged miners in other colonies—especially in Forbes, which had been burned a few days before Ludlow while the residents were out of the camp. Shouting "Remember Ludlow!" the Forbes strikers burned coal mining equipment, the post office, and other buildings, and slaughtered dozens of mules.[5]

The loss of the mules must have greatly troubled the mine operators.

CHAPTER TWENTY-SIX

Female Power in Action

MOURNERS STREAMED THROUGH THE STREETS of Trinidad all week. A fragile truce was declared, banning the militia from entering Trinidad while the dead of Ludlow were buried. Even so, a mysterious fire erupted in the morgue of the Hall-McMahon Funeral Home, and employees were compelled to rush the Ludlow caskets into the street. Once the flames were put out and the smoke cleared, the coffins were moved back inside.

Ludlow was destroyed on Monday, April 20. That Friday, James Fyler and Frank Rubino were buried. The next morning, Holy Trinity Church bells rang at nine o'clock as 1,500 miners and their families silently lined the streets in the weak spring sunshine for more funerals. There was no money for proper hearses, so mourners watched in shocked awe as the undertakers loaded fourteen coffins onto modest horse-drawn wagons. Three dark wood caskets contained the bodies of John Bartoloti, Mrs. Costa, and Mrs. Valdez. Eleven small white coffins cradled the young ones. A wagon bearing the body of Louis Tikas led the procession from Hall-McMahon Funeral Home to Holy Trinity Church and then on to their final resting place at the Catholic cemetery. Tikas's coffin was then returned to the mortuary to await the arrival of the Greek Orthodox priest.

That afternoon, people gathered again for Frank Snyder's funeral. Mourners observed that the undertakers had done an admirable job on Frank. As he lay peacefully in the casket, the only visible wound was a bruise above his eye where the bullet had entered his head.

In Denver that same morning, one thousand members of the Women's Peace Association stormed the governor's office, telling him, "The women of Denver summon you … do you understand?" He understood, but he avoided their delegation demanding that he telegraph President Wilson to ask that federal troops be sent to the southern Colorado coal fields. Sporadic acts of vengeance had broken out in Ludlow despite the truce, and the women's delegation assumed that more

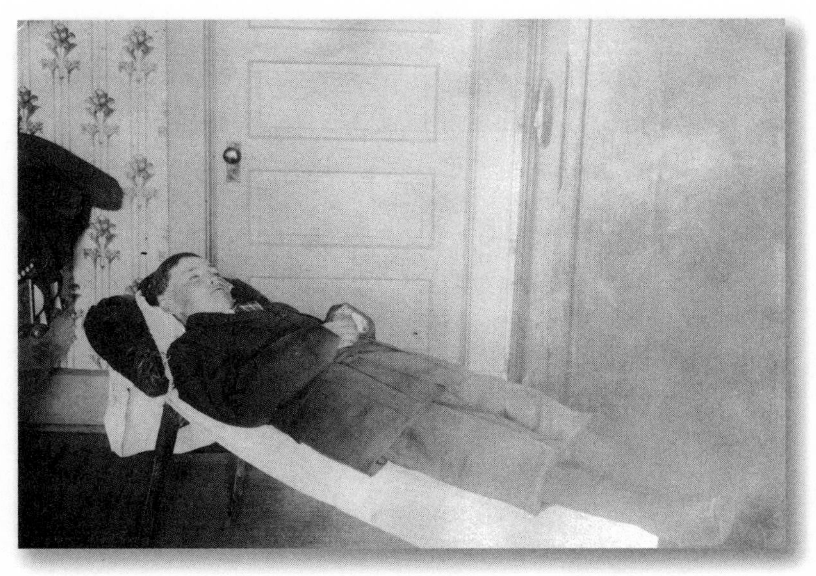

Frank Snyder was eleven years old when he was killed in the crossfire of the coal field war in Ludlow.

violence was to come. They were determined not to leave until the governor did what they asked. The day grew long and tedious, and their hymn singing gave way to a silent vigil. By nine o'clock that night, Governor Ammons had sent the telegram to Washington and an aide read it aloud to the weary but triumphant women.

A Denver newspaper called this sit-in one of the century's first examples of female power in action.[1]

And yet, that most powerful and influential of women, Mother Jones, was not there. It is curious how she had such enormous impact, yet was *not there* for so many of the most dramatic of Colorado's coal field moments. She'd been imprisoned in the Mount San Rafael Hospital while the Mother Jones Riot took place a few miles away in Trinidad. She'd been in Washington testifying at a congressional hearing when Ludlow erupted in flames. And during the Women's Peace Association siege of the statehouse she was in Denver but busy preparing for a massive demonstration to be held the next day. Mother Jones commanded a much larger stage.

So it was that on April 26, the day before Tikas was buried, she spoke to a crowd of five thousand huddled in the pouring rain and whipping winds on the grounds of the Colorado capitol. Some of the speakers who shared the podium with her called Governor Ammons a traitor and "accessory to **infanticide**."[2] As for Mother Jones, she stayed true to form. She bombarded the crowd with these familiar words that had served her well before, "Here I am again, boys, just back from Washington, and you aren't licked by a whole lot. Washington is aroused and there is help coming. Just keep your heads level and don't do anything to disgrace the state. The state is all right. It's just a few fools at the head of things that are bad."[3]

Later, Mother Jones boasted at the congressional investigation, "If I had been in Colorado ... this tragedy [Ludlow] would not have taken place."

Congressman Foster, who chaired the investigation, tried to clarify. "You think you could have prevented it?"

"I could have prevented it," Mother Jones responded with certainty.[4]

Setting aside her lack of humility, scholars doubt she could have stopped the spontaneous eruption of violence on April 20. In fact, some speculate that her **incendiary** speeches might have sparked an even larger conflagration. But that's another story.[5]

At that April gathering on the statehouse lawn, Mother Jones toned down her customary rhetoric with maternal advice. "Go home, boys. Mind me now and keep cool. Stay out of the saloons, save your money, and when I want you, I'll call you."[6]

They did not wait around for her call. Her words of caution were heeded only until Louis Tikas was buried.

CHAPTER TWENTY-SEVEN

The Ten Day War

MOTHER JONES'S TRAIN FROM DENVER arrived in Trinidad in time for Louis Tikas's funeral on Monday, April 27. Tikas's countrymen swore an oath of vengeance, pounding their rifle butts in four sharp blows to the floor of the chapel.

Amid incense, scented candles, and doleful chants, Father Paschopoulos led the funeral mass for Tikas and two other Greek men who had died in skirmishes with the militia at another tent colony. Three times the priest kissed Tikas's cheeks and anointed his forehead with wine and dust.

After the mass, Mother Jones walked with hundreds of mourners, all wearing black bands pinned to their sleeves. The mile-long funeral procession headed solemnly down Commercial Street, across the Purgatoire River bridge, and over the hill to the Knights of Pythias Cemetery, where Tikas was praised for his idealism and courage as a great leader.

Violence began with a vengeance after Tikas, the last of the Ludlow victims, was lowered into the earth and the gravediggers began reversing their somber work. The rebel-

The funeral procession of Louis Tikas as it passed through Trinidad, Colorado. Mother Jones walked with the hundreds of miners in the mile-long funeral procession.

lion came to be known as the Ten Day War. More than a thousand miners, some from as far away as Wyoming, tied red bandanas around their necks and shouted, "Remember Ludlow!" They occupied Trinidad, now rid of all militia. Las Animas County sheriff, Jim Grisham, and his deputies, barricaded themselves in the basement of the courthouse, expecting an attack.[1]

Open warfare erupted from Trinidad north to Walsenburg creating a forty-mile war zone. There are vivid reports of the miners throwing oil on CF&I equipment, shooting armed guards and scabs, and openly firing on the Colorado militia that had fled from Trinidad. Union supporters set fire to CF&I buildings within a 250-mile radius of the Ludlow Tent Colony. A band of Greeks outraged by Tikas's murder rushed in from all over Colorado and New Mexico to fight the militia. One report claims that more than 600 men, on both sides, died during the Ten Day War.[2]

General Chase's troops were reduced to about 250 men, and he was desperate to recruit more. He brought the new recruits from Denver to Trinidad on a special train.

The train had machine guns mounted on a flat car loaded with 500 rounds of shrapnel.[3] Sensing defeat, however, he called John Lawson, the UMW official who was the formal leader of Ludlow Tent Colony, to work out a truce in the interest of peace.

Lawson was not interested. He said, "There will be no peace when there is no justice. It is a war of extermination. ... We now have the faith, loyalty, and financial help of every union man in the country."[4]

While that might have been an exaggeration, by April 30 there was a call for a nationwide coal strike. Union leaders proclaimed, "Half a million miners have heard the death cries from Ludlow."[5] The threatened strike did not happen, but public awareness was aroused by five brave women. Ludlow survivors Mary Thomas, Pearl Jolly, Margaret Dominiski, and Mary Petrucci were joined by Mother Jones. She knew that miners' deaths would not attract national attention, but children's deaths would.[6] They began touring the country to speak out about what had happened at Ludlow.

The women picketed John D. Rockefeller Jr.'s New York City home and later criticized him at a massive meeting in New York's Beethoven Hall. They went to Washington to ask President Wilson to intervene in the strike that continued on for eight more months after the terrible events at Ludlow.

Mary Petrucci, who had lost her three children at Ludlow, was the most tragic and most courageous of these women. In an interview during the tour, she said, "We are working people, my husband and I—and we're stronger for the union than before the strike.... I can't have my babies back. But perhaps when everybody knows about this, something will be done to make the world a better place for all babies."[7]

CHAPTER TWENTY-EIGHT

President Wilson's Plan

"HAVE YOU CONSTITUTIONAL LAW AND GOVERNMENT in Colorado?" Reverend Atkinson, a Colorado minister, asked Governor Ammons.

The governor replied, "Not a bit in those counties where the coal mines are located."

Astounded, Rev. Atkinson tried to clarify the governor's position. "Do you mean to say that in large sections of your state there is no constitutional liberty?"

"Absolutely none," Governor Ammons replied.[1]

A congressional report released around the time of the Ten Day War speculated about the danger of a national revolution growing out of the Colorado strike. "Open insurrection," (rebellion) the governor called it, appealing to President Woodrow Wilson for federal troops.

To the humiliation of General Chase, federal troops were ordered to arrive on April 30 to do what Chase had failed to do—keep the peace. Chase would have to withdraw his entire militia and return to his Denver practice as an eye doctor. Miners welcomed the promised arrival of federal troops as an opportunity to end the strike. However, the new optimism didn't interfere with their final acts of vengeance and last-minute raids. Mother Jones pleaded with them to go home peaceably.

The on-site mine operators also got their last-minute assaults in before the federal troops arrived. They were set on punishing the strikers and their leaders, throwing many of them in the Huerfano and Las Animas County jails. They held mock trials by juries that were handpicked by the coal managers. One of these rigged juries went so far as to convict John Lawson of murder. He was the leader of the Ludlow colony and a high-ranking UMW official. Out on bail, Lawson continued working on the miners' behalf while waiting for a new trial in a real court of law. His case ended in dismissal of all charges, but not until three more years passed.[4]

Ten days after Ludlow, 350 members of the Second Squadron, Fifth U.S. Cavalry Regiment arrived at the Trinidad train depot.[2] Governor Ammons immediately asked for more men, and another 1,600 soldiers soon followed. Mine operators feared that President Wilson would take their properties and nationalize coal production, as Mother Jones had urged. "Coal is a mineral. … No coal company on the face of the earth made it," she once said. "It belongs to the nation. It was there down through the ages and it belongs to every generation."[3]

President Wilson was determined to do more than just send troops into Colorado. In order to end the strike, he offered a proposal for both sides of the dispute to consider. It had its drawbacks.[5] Wilson's plan included:

- a three-year truce, meaning no gunfire and no strikes or demonstrations by union workers
- an agreement that there would be no bullying of either union or nonunion workers in the mines

- a strict enforcement of Colorado's mining and labor laws, although no system was in place to enforce the laws
- rehiring miners who'd been fired for union activity, provided they hadn't violated laws
- the creation of a grievance committee for each mine, selected by the miners, and if that group couldn't come to a compromise, the dispute would be referred to an arbitration board appointed by President Wilson. The board would listen to all sides and make a decision that miners and managers alike would have to accept. However, there was a catch. Only men employed six months or more could serve on the grievance committee. This meant that only scabs would be eligible to serve on a grievance committee since most miners had been out on strike longer than six months.
- mine guards would no longer be employed, but there was no ban on mine "watchmen." It was hard to see any difference between the two.

The plan did not address working hours, safety conditions, or higher pay. In fact, officials of the southern Colorado UMW district, saw nothing in President Wilson's plan that would help their striking members. But the union was out of money, and the workers were out of spirit, and even Mother Jones, who was never fond of compromising, recommended accepting the flawed proposal.

In the end, the plan was rejected by both the union and the mine operators. Mother Jones made a trip to Washington in October in a last-ditch effort to get President Wilson to close the mines if the mine operators refused to accept at least some of Wilson's proposals. The president replied that he didn't have the authority to either close or nationalize the mines. Most miners returned to work in defeat, even though the strike dragged on for three more crippling months.

The world beyond the Colorado coal fields was in turmoil. World War I had begun in August 1914, disrupting American industry. Prices for everyday necessities skyrocketed. As Winter 1914 approached, four million people were without jobs, and several million more had only part-time work.[6,7]

Having no alternative, the miners voted to end the strike on December 14, 1914. Frank Hayes, a high-ranking union official, said glumly, "Thus passed into history one of the greatest conflicts ever waged by any body of workers on this continent."[8]

Nothing really changed in the miners' working conditions after fifteen months of strife and many deaths. The one alarming difference was that the union could no longer provide support for the men who were refused jobs as punishment for striking. Many miners drifted out of Colorado to look for work elsewhere, but jobs everywhere were hard to come by.

Mother Jones carried on her fight for better working conditions for miners, and she still drew crowds when she gave a speech. Thousands gathered in New York to hear her mocking and simplistic evaluation of the long strike: "The union lost in Colorado ... because on their side the workers had only the Constitution. The other side had bayonets. In the end bayonets always win."[9]

CHAPTER TWENTY-NINE

Massacre or Not?

REAL LIFE ISN'T TELEVISION. On TV everything is tied up neatly at the end when the credits roll. Three nagging questions will probably never be resolved in the story of Ludlow. Conflicting evidence abounds on both sides of these questions, as in most issues involving Mother Jones.

(1) Who were the good guys (the victims), and who were the bad guys (the villains)?

(2) Who fired the first shot?

(3) Was the Ludlow Massacre truly a "massacre"?

Maybe the answers don't really matter, considering the ghastly outcome. But because a robust battle of wits was Mother Jones's way of looking for truth, let's take a moment to think about each question.

(1) Who were the victims, and who were the villains?

At first glance, it seems obvious that the miners were the victims. They were denied the right to organize under the union, they were powerless to change the unsafe, unfair conditions under which they worked, while supervised by harsh guards and detectives. Once they declared the strike, their living conditions worsened, their poverty increased, and many miners ended up in the bullpen on trumped-up charges. When the situation turned into warfare, they were at first outnumbered by a better equipped militia. Yet, the warring miners were like freedom fighters in an armed resistance against an unjust system, and they won the war, though not the strike itself.[1]

On the other hand, mine operators had a responsibility to keep the mines working, even if it meant hiring scabs. The nation needed coal for the growing industries and transportation, even more so as World War I got under way. Mine owners, such as Rockefeller, were thought to be concerned only with adding to their own wealth, which appeared to be their reason for denying union organization within the mines. The mine owners seemed to give no thought to the human beings digging coal thousands of feet underground, or of families trying to survive on low wages.

In fairness, Rockefeller and his colleagues truly believed that unions sabotaged the American economy and production. They, the owners and operators, and not the unions, were obliged to listen to grievances and make necessary changes, if the miners continued to provide an honest day's labor. The owners didn't understand why mining families resented the convenience of the company store or the fact that credit was extended to them to meet their daily needs.

Rockefeller and his cohorts took a paternalistic view common to the situation. A paternalistic view can be explained like this: The mine owner is the father, the head of this family of laborers. It's his responsibility to provide meaningful work and whatever the laborer needs in the way of food, shelter, housing, medicine, education, and moral training. If the miner is a loyal, efficient worker, both he and the owner prosper. If the miner's wife is supportive of the mine owners, the miner's family thrives. If the miners and their families act like good boys and girls, all goes smoothly. Nobody gets taken out to the woodshed. But if they don't behave, there are consequences. Everyone should try to get along as one big, happy family.

Paternalism had worked for generations, even as the world grew more industrialized and workers grew more aware of their rights. The owners were genuinely perplexed. Why wasn't it working now?

Who were the victims, who the villains? "[I]gnorance and braggadocio affected the strikers to a reckless degree," and union leaders sometimes had their own agendas separate from the needs of the miners. The same could be said about the mine operators. Leaders on both sides of the conflict were "straitjacked (held back) by principles and prejudices."[2]

(2) Who fired the first shot at Ludlow? The strikers had been on watch all Sunday night, ever since the confrontation earlier that day at the baseball game during the Orthodox Easter celebration. There'd been five armed and belligerent militiamen on the field making vague, hostile threats. ("That's right, girlie, you have your big Sunday today and tomorrow we will have the roast ... ")[3]

By Monday morning, the miners were in a heightened state of alert, guns oiled and loaded, as they watched the militiamen getting into position above them on Water Tank Hill. Machine guns were pointed at the tent colony. Most of the militia had been withdrawn, and only a few hundred militiamen remained, massed and ready on Cedar Hill, and now they were outnumbered by the strikers' redneck army. Many of the strikers had fought in wars before they'd left Europe; they were young, spirited, angry, and chomping to fight.

A spy for the mine operators learned that the Ludlow men were planning an attack, and they were heavily armed and primed for battle. The militia thought that, given the chance, the strikers would overtake the militia, seize the mines, and take revenge on the hated scabs and mine guards.

It was a rumor, probably planted to justify a defensive attack by the militia. Three rather harmless explosives had been hurled toward the colony. The militia later testified that these bombs were fired to summon support from Cedar Hill, in the event of an attack from the miners.

That was not how the Ludlow men interpreted it. They saw the explosives as a direct attack. Enraged, the strikers fired, or fired back. And so it began. Gunfire rained down from Cedar Hill; Ludlow women and children ran for cover; and finally, tents turned to ash, whether accidentally by the gunfire or by deliberate torching.

So, who fired the first shot? In truth, sporadic shots had been fired from both sides for months. Maybe there was no "first shot" at all on the day Ludlow perished.

(3) Was the Ludlow Massacre truly a "massacre"? The ongoing archaeological digs done by the Colorado Coal Field War Project may eventually resolve this question.[4] Students and professors from the University of Denver and Fort Lewis College continue to study the Ludlow Tent Colony's trash pits—rich ground for archaeologists. They've unearthed bullets that landed in the tent colony and a coffee pot shot through with bullets. They've also found cartridges that had been discharged by strikers within the colony. Parts of shotguns have been found at the site of the tent colony. Shotguns would have been handy for hunting rabbits and possums but not much defense against the militia's machine guns and high-powered rifles.

In a heated conference at Colorado College in April 2009, one professor posed the issue this way: "The United

Mine Workers of America, having successfully spun the death of the striking miner families as a *massacre*, may have made an unmerited impact on the public's sympathies." The professor continued, "but likewise, deciding to call Ludlow *not a massacre* will be falsely charged, as well."[5] (As early as May 11, 1914, John D. Rockefeller Jr., in an investigative hearing, referred to the events as the Ludlow Massacre.)

The *Oxford English Dictionary* defines *massacre* as carnage, slaughter, and the cruel and violent killing of people in large numbers. When all the killings during the 1913–1914 coal strike were tallied, the death toll on both sides was seventy-five.[6] The strikers suffered twenty-five casualties for each one of the casualties among the militia.[7]

Intentional killing and collateral damage were not new to labor conflicts, nor did they end with Ludlow and its aftermath. If it were only National Guardsmen and strikers who died, would Ludlow be called a massacre? Wouldn't losing these fighters be expected during a battle? More likely, the word *massacre* has been applied to Ludlow because of the mothers and children who suffocated underground rather than to men shot down in battle. There is no evidence that the militiamen who burned the tent colony knew that anyone was below ground. If "intention to kill" is key to the definition of the term *massacre*, then the loss of life beneath the tents—as horrific and tragic as it was—would not meet that definition.

Arguing this point, Ludlow has been described as an unfortunate incident, as a battle, or as negligent homicide. Historian Scott Martelle points out that in his opinion, the true massacre was the deliberate assassination of Louis Tikas and two other men while the tents were set aflame.[8]

Was Ludlow truly a massacre? Yes … and no.

CHAPTER THIRTY

Rockefeller Has a Plan

THIRTEEN PEOPLE, ELEVEN OF THEM CHILDREN, all suffocating in a pit under burning tents. Never could such a thing happen in America!

Mother Jones spread the word, and Americans were rattled out of their indifference about the horrific conditions under which miners and their families lived and died. When Mary Thomas, Margaret Dominiski, and Mary Petrucci, who'd lost three children in that underground oven, courageously traversed the country speaking about the tragedy, Americans listened. They began to recognize for the first time "corporate power enforced at the point of a gun on one side, [and] American citizens impoverished and deprived of civil liberties on the other."[1]

Within a few weeks after the strike ended, Mother Jones testified before the U.S. Commission on Industrial Relations. She was "one of the most entertaining witnesses.... Not a question interrupted her and she proceeded in her quaint way without being tied down to geography or continuity of events."[2] Even so, she described in detail the horrors within the mines and tents. Again she advocated for the impossible.

That the federal government take control of mining. It was not going to happen.

A few positive actions grew out of public response to the southern Colorado coal field war. Mine operators were compelled to make some adjustments. Later in 1914, miners began to see slightly better compensation for injuries or death from accidents caused by "defective machinery, tools, or plant facilities that the employer should have corrected through ordinary diligence."[3] Cases against the companies were hard to prove, however.

Meanwhile, public opinion turned against Rockefeller. The investigating commission revealed inhumane practices in his mines. Many were in conflict with state laws and all were harmful to mine employees. Rockefeller might have been able to ignore the commission, but heavy financial losses caused him to announce that he would take steps to "prevent possible recurrence at any time in the future of the disorder and loss … which has resulted from the recent strike."[4]

In 1915 he developed the Rockefeller Plan, which came to be called the Colorado Plan. In each of CF&I's five districts, committees composed of equal numbers of managers and miners would meet. Together, they would address issues related to wages, safety, sanitation, health, housing, recreation, education, election of check-weighmen, and industrial cooperation. It was a tall order.

The plan sounded promising, although Mother Jones called it a sham and a fraud, and warned Rockefeller, "You can't fool my boys. They know that this kind of scheme is a hypocritical and dishonest practice."[5]

The Colorado Plan *did* prevent some bitterness, but in truth, the company still maintained most of the control and refused to recognize the union for collective bargaining. The plan netted some small gains in welfare, medical care, housing, and education, but those gains were granted to the workers *by* management rather than negotiated *with* the miners.[6] Industry paternalism still flourished, as did the miners' grievances. During the first seven years the Colorado Plan was in effect, there were seven coal mine strikes, four of which involved CF&I.

In 1921, CF&I discontinued the wage increases it had granted. Nevertheless, the spirit of the plan may have paved the way for greater gains in unionizing down the road. Eighteen years into the plan, it was abandoned when miners overwhelmingly voted for an independent union to represent their interests. CF&I had no choice but to negotiate its first genuine collective bargaining agreement with the United Mine Workers.

Hard-won victory, at last.

As for Mother Jones, she was not directly involved with the Colorado Plan. She visited Colorado and brought money and clothes and food to miners trying to get back on their feet after the strike, but she'd moved on to other ventures, perhaps to make up for what she recognized as losses in Colorado. She was not one to lose gracefully.

Mother Jones traveled continuously between 1915 and 1917, even as World War I raged on. She was on the West Coast organizing steelworkers. In October 1915, she incited a huge group of striking immigrant garment workers in Chicago. That rally ended in police beatings and numerous arrests, but the Amalgamated Clothing Workers of America won a major victory for higher pay, a shorter workweek, and—perhaps most prized—union recognition.

In Pittsburgh, she led ten thousand steelworkers in a parade after union meetings were forbidden. By December 1917, sixty thousand steel workers joined the union and promptly began a massive strike. Mother Jones was there among them, Colorado all but forgotten.

People who have studied Mother Jones and the dozens of strikes she plunged into, before and after Ludlow, suggest that the conflict in southern Colorado was "the most demanding and violent strike in which she played a part."[7]

CHAPTER THIRTY-ONE

At Death's Door

AGE HAD SLOWED MOTHER JONES DOWN BY THE 1920'S. Even so, now well into her eighties, she made two trips to Mexico. In Chicago, she threw herself into a four-month dressmakers' strike. In 1922–1923 alone, she traveled to West Virginia, California, Indiana, Michigan, New York, Washington, D.C., and Colorado to help organize unions in all those places.

She wrote to various friends that she was suffering so badly with rheumatism that she could barely hold a pen and struggled with the words and spelling: "Since I saw yo(u) I have been at Death's Door. If I had not been with such loyal friends, I would be sleeping in the Clay long before this. … I have so much to say, but my hand Trembles."[1]

Receiving such a letter in 1921, just before Mother Jones left for one of her campaigns in Mexico, Terence Powderly responded, "I ask you to always bear in mind that there is only one Mother Jones. I doubt if the world has seen her like before and while I hope for the future, sadly feel the world will not see her like again."[2]

In fact, the world saw her for nine more years. In 1923 she wrote her autobiography. Her collaborator, journalist

Mary Field Parton, took the stories Mother Jones spun and tried to show what they meant at the time. The *Autobiography of Mother Jones* is a spirited and sparkling slice of her public life and opinions, but it is certainly not the whole picture or the most accurate account of her vast experiences.

Ronnie Gilbert wrote a play about the controversial and slippery Mary Harris Jones. The play was titled *Mother Jones: Face to Face with the Most Dangerous Woman in America.* In her preface to the script, Gilbert wrote, "It would be unkind and untrue to conclude that Mother Jones was a liar.... I would say she was one of that talented breed of great storytellers who would never let the absolute truth spoil a good yarn."[3]

Mother Jones despaired about the declining strength of labor unions. In 1922 she wrote in a letter, "I see that Colorado is gone, Utah is gone, New Mexico is gone, Alabama is gone, and I am afraid it is going to be long years to build up your organization in West Virginia."[4]

West Virginia endured a particularly contentious and bloody strike in 1921–1922. Mother Jones was right in the midst of it. She had given a good portion of her energies to West Virginia and had been jailed there many times over the previous twenty years. Now she saw "her boys" sorely defeated and demoralized. It must have seemed that her efforts had been fruitless. She never returned to West Virginia.

It was Colorado, however, that plagued her most. In 1924 she wrote, "Things do not look very favorable in the West to me. I had a letter from Denver stating that things were in bad shape."[5] A year later she said, "They have a hard time in Colorado. The Ku Klux [Klan] control the whole state now. ... I am afraid they are going to create a great deal of trouble before they are done away with."[6]

THE KU KLUX KLAN IN COLORADO

In the mid-1920s, Colorado was in the control of the Ku Klux Klan, which was anti-minorities, anti-Jewish, and anti-Catholic. These sentiments were common throughout the nation, but Colorado was especially hard-hit. As the *Denver Post* wrote, "Beyond any doubt the KKK is the largest and most cohesive, most efficiently organized political force in the state." Under the charismatic leadership of John Galen Locke, the Klan managed to get one of their own elected governor, along with a majority of the state legislators. Governor Clarence Morley took office in 1926. When his term ended, he opened a stock brokerage firm in Indiana and was soon indicted for mail fraud. He spent five years in Leavenworth Prison.

For more on Clarence Morley and the KKK in Colorado, see http://www.colorado.gov/dpa/doit/archives/govs/morley.html

Mother Jones's letters between 1900 and 1930 reflected her disillusionment with the growing corruption in the UMW. As she grew older, she had had differences with the UMW leadership, and now she was discouraged with the state of labor organizing in general. Still, she managed to conjure up a modest degree of optimism. In a 1922 letter to William Green, secretary-treasurer of the UMW from 1912 to 1924, she wrote, "I know you cannot do all that your heart beats and throbs to do, but anyhow ... let us keep up courage and the future probably will be ours."[7] Note the word *probably*. How different this sounds from what she said in an interview a decade earlier, "Why, I'm so great an optimist that some people may regard me as a dreamer."[8]

Mother Jones wasn't entirely grim in her outlook during her later years. She told reporters that she'd lived to earn the title of "grandmother of agitators," and she was looking forward to being the "great-grandmother of agitators." In

1928 she said, "I will be ninety-nine the first day of next May and I want to live to be a hundred and come to Chicago to celebrate the anniversary."[9]

She did or did not live to be a hundred, depending on which year you believe she was born. At a birthday celebration in 1930, she would have only been ninety-three if historians are correct about her birth year being 1837. But no one quibbled over the count. Her declining health and partial blindness prevented her from going to Chicago, where the party was to be held. She had been in and out of consciousness over the past year, and virtually bedridden. She remained in the care of friends Lillie May and Walter Burgess on their farm in Hyattsville, Maryland.

The party was moved to Maryland. As the ancient saying goes, if the mountain won't come to Muhammed, Muhammed must go to the mountain. Scores of people, perhaps as many as a thousand, came by special buses and trains from all over the nation to celebrate with Mother Jones. When she was escorted from her room to the front lawn, the crowd fell silent. Union officials, dignitaries, and "her boys," the common laborers, removed their hats in reverence for the grandmother of agitators. All watched her cut into the five-tiered birthday cake glowing with a hundred flaming candles.

She was in glorious form that day. Bundled in a blanket under a shady apple tree, she held court in the manner of a queen. Even as the light in her own eyes dimmed, she relished the limelight. She gave interviews, made some of her feisty statements, and affirmed the influence of women in the future of the country. She also entertained everyone with stories of all the advancements she'd lived through. Having grown up before the Civil War, she'd heard President Lincoln speak in person. She'd seen horse-drawn carriages

Mother Jones celebrated her one-hundredth birthday in 1930, even though it is unlikely that she was born in 1830. Most scholars agree that she was born in 1837.

give way to automobiles, which she called "delightful contraptions." She'd marveled at the invention of electric lights and trains that crossed the entire country. She'd lived long enough to see federal child labor laws passed. Now, on her one hundredth birthday, she gazed into the camera of a Paramount News team for an interview in the newfangled "talkies."[10]

Among the thousands of cards, letters, and telegrams Mother Jones received, perhaps the most amazing was from John D. Rockefeller Jr. His telegram read, in part, "Please accept my heartiest congratulations on your 100th birthday. Your loyalty to your ideals, your fearless adherence to your duty as you have seen it, is an inspiration to all who have known you." His words were carefully chosen, conceding no blame and yielding no territory to her.

Her words in response were not so polite. "Well, he's a damn good sport, anyway. We surely had some bitter battles. But it was kind of him to remember me, but hell, I can't do him or anyone any harm for I'm out of the running now."[11]

She was, indeed, out of the running. Six months later, November 30, 1930, she died in her sleep. What was most remarkable about her death was that she had no final statement to shout to the world.

CHAPTER THIRTY-TWO

National Landmark

In southern Colorado coal country lies sacred ground—a forty-acre field halfway between Trinidad, where the Mother Jones Riot erupted, and Walsenburg, where she spent twenty-six days isolated in a dungeon. The United Mine Workers had purchased the land where Ludlow Tent Colony had once stood. On April 20, 1917, the third anniversary of the Ludlow Massacre, a crowd gathered and stood beside the underground pit where the thirteen had suffocated. A union official dropped flowers into that dark chasm as a band played "Nearer My God to Thee."[1]

The gathering was called to commemorate the dead and to plan a monument to honor the miners' sacrifices during the strike. A week later, just as the union was beginning to collect donations for the monument, another catastrophe occurred at Hastings Mine, across the prairie a few miles west of Ludlow. Eight thousand feet deep into the mine, an explosion killed 121 miners; their bodies were never recovered. Perhaps the magnitude of this tragedy encouraged southern Colorado miners to dig deeper into their pockets, even though they were still struggling to earn a living. Somehow $12,000 was collected, and the following year, thousands of people returned for the dedication of a monument to those lost at Ludlow.

On that triumphant day, May 30, 1918, special trains, automobiles, and wagons carried hordes of people from Trinidad and southern Colorado farms and towns to the windy, open field. A dozen bands played. Five thousand people marched in a parade, each waving a small American flag and wearing the red bandana that was the symbol of striking miners. At the head of the parade, a man carried the shredded flag of Ludlow colony along with a new flag symbolizing justice. Speakers addressed the crowd in several languages. Some dropped flowers into the gaping hole in which the women and children had sought safety when the colony was set afire four years earlier.

In their midst loomed the eighteen-foot-high granite monument blanketed in an American flag. Mary Petrucci had the honor of removing the flag to reveal a life-size figure of a miner standing proud and tall, gazing off toward the coal mounds. A step above his feet sits his wife, cradling a child. She is looking away, perhaps symbolizing their different roles—his to work in the mines, and hers to nurture home and family. An unexpected and, for the most part, unrecognized spectator in the day's activities was John D. Rockefeller Jr. Mother Jones, however, was not present.

In 2003, vandals broke off the stone heads of the miner and his wife. Within two years, union supporters worldwide had paid to have the monument restored. Today, the stairs and walls of the hole are fortified with cement. Visitors can climb down into the cold pit. When the door is closed, they can imagine what it must have felt like for those children and their mothers in the deep, dark underground, with little hope of escaping the flames, smoke, and gunfire above them.

A monument to those who died during the labor war that came to be called The Ludlow Massacre rises on the site of the Ludlow Tent Colony.

In the summer of 2009, almost one hundred years after that deadly day, the U.S. Department of Interior designated Ludlow a National Historic Landmark. Though ripe with grim memories, the occasion was nevertheless joyous and electrifying. Gone were the special trains of the last century. In the twenty-first century, hundreds of cars wedged their way into the fields surrounding the monument. Car doors flew open in the prairie wind and spilled out seven hundred men, women, and children from all over North America. They gathered under a huge tent to honor the dead and to celebrate the solidarity of union supporters. Colorado governor Bill Ritter spoke, as did at least a dozen other spirited men and women, though none were as fiery-tongued as Mother Jones once was.

A key speaker was Dr. Elizabeth Jameson. She had spearheaded the five-year mission to designate this sacred ground as a National Historic Landmark. A representative of the U.S. Department of Interior presented an official plaque to dedicate Ludlow as a monument to be remembered forever.

A special elderly guest in the front row rose and faced the crowd when he was introduced. Frank Petrucci, proudly decked out in his old union jacket, was born to Mary Petrucci after the Ludlow Massacre. He was one of the few people still alive with close connections to Ludlow survivors. Many in the crowd wiped away tears as he made a brief, humble speech and waved shyly.

Mother Jones's name came up at least a dozen times during the dedication. For many miners and their wives and children, Mary Harris Jones continued to be the inspiration, the call to action, and the very heart of their courageous sacrifices since the strike of 1913–1914. Each time her name was mentioned, the excited crowd responded with wild applause, foot-stomping, and cheering, affirming that she remains the heart and soul of the miners' union. If anyone doubts that statement, here's a bit of support.

Miners of the Pittston Coal Company, in Virginia's Appalachian mountain country, struggled through a strike from April 1989 to June 1990. In the middle of it, forty miners' wives occupied the company's offices for a day and a half, protesting the harsh conditions under which their husbands labored. Interviewed years later, one leader of that sit-in recalled, "If somebody would say 'I'm tired,' we would say, 'Mother Jones, there was times she would be tired.... If we've got to go to jail and pull time, we will. Mother Jones did.'"[2] Eventually police arrested the women, who called themselves Daughters of Mother Jones.

CHAPTER THIRTY-THREE

Eighty Tons of Granite

MARY "MOTHER" JONES
BORN MAY 1, 1830
DIED NOVEMBER 30, 1930
"SHE GAVE HER LIFE TO THE WORLD OF LABOR,
HER BLESSED SOUL TO HEAVEN.
GOD'S FINGER TOUCHED HER—
AND NOW SHE SLEEPS."

SO READS THE MARKER NEAR HER GRAVE in the Union Miners Cemetery in Mount Olive, Illinois. Earlier in the twentieth century, many cemeteries refused to receive the bodies of miners involved in labor strikes. Residents of Mount Olive bought the small plot of land for a special miners' grave site, dedicated to the martyrs of an 1898 bloody union battle called the Virden Massacre.

Beginning in 1903, Mother Jones made many pilgrimages to this spot to pay tribute to the fallen Virden men. They had gone on strike against the operators of the mine. African American strikebreakers were brought in to keep the mine open. When the scabs realized they'd have to cross a picket line, most refused to work and chose to get back on the trains to go home. But the mine operators threatened to shoot them if they didn't go to work—and the striking miners refused to let them enter the mines. The National Guard was called in, violence escalated, and a few strikebreakers and twenty-four striking miners died. Four of the miners were buried in the Mount Olive cemetery.

Although Mother Jones wasn't involved in the Virden strike, it was her fervent wish to be buried with the men who'd been killed in that Illinois battle. Late in her life she said, "It will be my consolation when I pass away, to feel that I sleep under the clay with those brave boys."[1]

In keeping with her zeal for drama, she'd planned her own funeral. She didn't want an elaborate casket, just a plain metal one, trusting that thousands of admirers would provide in her death the pomp and theatrics that she craved in life. A High Requiem Mass was celebrated in Washington, D.C. The eight pallbearers represented different trade unions. Her body was transported to St. Louis by a special car of the Baltimore and Ohio Railroad, and a second train took her body the forty miles to Mount Olive.

Her coffin was open for viewing at Odd Fellows Hall. A rosary was "entwined in her withered fingers," and it is said that she was buried in a lavender dress.[2] How odd this must have looked to her admirers who'd only seen her in her customary black, dusty-hemmed widow's gown!

Red and gold union flags decorated her casket, which was set below a picture of herself and the four martyrs of the Virden Massacre who were already buried at Mount Olive. Nearly fifteen thousand people passed by her coffin and attended a memorial service at the Church of the Ascension in Mount Olive. A tinny, crackly loudspeaker broadcast the entire service for the benefit of the thousands of union supporters and journalists from around the country who couldn't fit into the small sanctuary.

She was laid to rest in the Union Miners Cemetery along side the miners she called "my boys." A plain gravestone simply reads, MOTHER MARY JONES.

America loves her heroes and pledges never to forget them, even those with the kind of contradictory reputations that Mother Jones enjoyed. Think of monuments like Mount Rushmore, the Lincoln Memorial, the Iwo Jima Memorial, and the Vietnam Memorial Wall with the names of fifty-eight thousand veterans etched in black granite.

Besides building evocative monuments, Americans also explore places that were important in their time. We also visit their burial sites, to solemnly reflect on the values and actions by which the heroes lived and died. Exhibits in museums breathe new life into nearly- forgotten lives.

Mother Jones is remembered in *all* of these ways and more, validating her importance in American history. In 1922 her name appeared in *The Nation* magazine as one of the twelve greatest American women.[3] Some admirers went so far as to declare her the most important woman in America in the early years of the twentieth century.

If you go to the National Women's Hall of Fame in Seneca Falls, New York, you'll see pictures, artifacts, and fascinating details about her life. Mother Jones would not be impressed to know that she was inducted into the Women's Hall of Fame fifty-four years after her death, considering her conflicted attitude toward women. She *would* be pleased to know that she's in the Labor Hall of Fame in Washington, D.C., which honors ordinary workers, because it is with common laborers that her life's energy and passion were centered.

One way that Mary Harris Jones's name has been preserved is in the publication of a magazine called *Mother Jones*, which has been published monthly since 1974. Although it has no ties to labor or unions, it chose its name out of admiration for the uncompromising way Mother Jones trudged fearlessly through life. Like her, the magazine is unflinching in its articles on political and social justice issues and embraces its role in the proud American tradition of journalistic muckraking.

The most eye-catching monument to Mother Jones is in the Mount Olive cemetery. It's built of eighty tons of pink

Mother Jones's monument is the most impressive in the Union Miners Cemetery in Mount Olive, Illinois, where she is buried among 'her boys.'

Minnesota granite and juts twenty-two feet into the air. About a third of the way down from the top is a circular bronze bas-relief portrait of Mother Jones. Below it are clasped hands symbolizing solidarity across all racial, ethnic, and class lines. Two life-size bronze coal miners, each clutching the tools of his trade, seem to be guarding Mother Jones in eternity, just as she'd looked after them in life.

On the day of the monument's dedication in 1936, it took five special trains and twenty-five Greyhound buses to bring fifty thousand people to the little town, located on historic Route 66. Others found their way on foot to Mount Olive and its cornfield cemetery.

Well into the twentieth century, people continued to gather at the monument each October 12 for Mother Jones Day. Today, tourists veer off the beaten path from Springfield, Illinois, to stand in awe at the foot of the monument to Mary Harris "Mother" Jones.

There is yet another monument to her. It's not made of granite or bronze, but some music historians claim that the popular song, "She'll Be Coming Round the Mountain," is about Mother Jones comin' 'round the Appalachian Mountains to help the coal miners of West Virginia. If the song is about her, it's a sure bet that she won't be "drivin' six white horses" or "wearin' red pajamas" when she comes 'round the mountain.

CHAPTER THIRTY-FOUR

Legacy

Sleep on—sleep on—the crusader of work well done,
Rest on—rest on—thy battles have been won.

THESE WORDS ARE FROM A POEM ABOUT MOTHER JONES, written by George Patrick Dooley. But have her battles really been won? The angel of the miners actually lost more coal field battles than she won, and most of her victories weren't gained in her lifetime. Measuring what she accomplished and passed on to future generations is tricky.

If her intent, in part, was to save children endangered by working in unsafe mills and mines, what about Frank Snyder, the eleven-year-old-boy who was shot through the head at Ludlow? What about hundreds of children whose bodies and spirits were crushed with labor too early in their lives?

If her intent was to secure safer working conditions in the mines, yet just west of Ludlow, in April 1917, a safety inspector eight thousand feet deep in the Hastings Mine re-lit his headlamp. The tiny spark from the lamp ignited coal dust in a pocket of gases and set off a massive explosion that killed 121 miners. Many of the bodies weren't removed for seven more months, and some were never recovered.[1]

Estimates are that seventy-five people went to their graves during the strike in southern Colorado. Did the gains outweigh the losses? Asking that question in 1914 or 1915 might have evoked a variety of answers:

"Sure it was worth it," a coal miner says. "It was fourteen horrific months of starvation and gunfire, but look what we gained."

"Nothing," his wife snaps. "You're still going down into those wretched mines with no safeguards, and you never see daylight from sun up to sun down. The kids and I listen for the warning siren and don't know if you're coming back up at all."

"At least I got my old job back, and we're eating. God bless Mother Jones, she's won us lots more solidarity among the guys."

"Solidarity? Fiddlesticks. It's still illegal for the union to organize."

If we'd heard that conversation in 1915, we'd conclude that the strike was not worth it. The UMW was crushed in Colorado and weakened throughout the nation—despite the sacrifices of thousands of miners' families and the heroic efforts of Mother Jones. It was only World War I that increased the demand for coal and opened the doorway to slightly greater union activity.

Or perhaps a different conversation might be overheard:

"Everybody's talking all over the country about the massacre at Ludlow. Those mine guard thugs and butchers, they'll be held accountable for what they did to us, you can bet on it."

"Oh, yeah? Our guys were just as bad, sometimes. Mother Jones lit a fuse under our feet and talked us into arming ourselves and fighting like men. We did, all right, we sure did."

Though Mother Jones was once called "the notorious apostle of violence," she went on record as saying, "Violence will never cure our labor troubles."[2] "I hate violence. I favor drama."[3] Typical of her contradictions, she also gave a speech in which she vividly described how violence sometimes succeeded as a strike weapon.[4] Most often, her speeches inflamed the workers and roused them to fury. There were times when they stormed out of the hall and into a street riot.

"No doubt Mother Jones was very skillful at working a crowd up to the edge of militant action," Elliot Gorn, her biographer, wrote: "Occasionally she did advocate spilling blood, though usually her words fell short of straightforward incitement to violence."[5] She often urged miners to arm themselves in self-defense, to be ready if the mine guards or militia shot at them. What the miners heard and what they did might have been two different things. At times, they took Mother Jones's warning words a step too far.

There were two extensive federal investigations of the Ludlow Massacre, one held on-site and in Washington, D.C., in 1914, and the other held entirely in Washington, a year later. In those hearings, the dire work conditions in the mines were revealed, along with the shocking violence on both sides of the armed conflict. Everyone thought they knew what had happened and who was to blame. Yet, of the 408 striking miners who had been charged with felonies, few went to court, and many had the charges against them dropped. Four were convicted, but all of the convictions were overturned. Meanwhile, on the other side of the enemy line, all the National Guard soldiers were either acquitted or had their cases overturned, despite overwhelming evidence that they were guilty. What's more, Mother Jones had campaigned vigorously to have Rockefeller's mine operators and guards fired, but not a single one lost his job.

Wait a minute! Give her a break! Mother Jones was fiercely dedicated. She was courageous. She took action. Look how she brought us food and shoes and money when we were so far down and out. Look how hard she worked to mold us into a community—all us immigrants talking a couple dozen languages, getting together with all the black and white Americans. Wouldn't have happened without her, right?

Creating community was one of her great strengths. As Elliot Gorn said, "Solidarity was not just a union slogan but a culture, a way of life, one that rejected America's worship of individualism and embraced instead the community of labor."[6]

No matter what we lost—life and limb—even the whole blasted strike, Mother Jones gave us the one thing we needed most. Hope. No one can take that away from us. Ever.

Hope is elusive. You can't wear it or eat it, and it won't keep you warm when the thermometer drops below zero. It is powerful, nevertheless. Mother Jones gave people the emotional support they desperately needed in their struggles. She convinced them to hold on and hold out, and that their aspirations for change were in the tradition of American idealism. One of her favorite expressions was, "We'll come out all right, boys." In very real, tangible terms, Mother Jones delivered, if not immediately then over time. To quote biographer Elliot Gorn, "Hundreds of thousands of American workers fought for and received better wages and working conditions during her years of activism, and they embraced a renewed ideal of democratic citizenship."[7]

Three years after her death, Congress passed the National Industrial Recovery Act of 1933. The law made it illegal for mine operators to interfere with union organizing. Admittedly, the law was hard to enforce and required another law two years later to boost its effectiveness. But the result was a huge increase in union activity and collective bargaining, which helped to change the lives of thousands of workers across the nation.

Mother Jones lay in her grave for thirty-nine years before the Mine Safety Act of 1969 came into law. It did much to protect miners from roof cave-ins, fires, and the kind of coal dust explosion that occurred at Hastings. Since then, in 1973, 1977, and 2006, additional federal laws have strengthened safeguards in the mines and drastically reduced mining fatalities.[8]

At last, the saplings Mother Jones planted in the earth have borne sweet fruit.

Epilogue

PICTURE MOTHER JONES SITTING on that prison hospital bed way back in 1914, her face buried in her hands and a blanket wrapped around her shoulders. She's scratching out a memo to herself. What to write?

Those high-class burglars and pirates, how'm I going to make 'em understand that they can't treat my boys like beasts of burden and starve their families? How'm I going to give my boys and girls the courage to stick it out through the miserable winter, on four paltry dollars a week? What's the first thing I have to do when they let me out of this military bastille? I'll head right back into Trinidad, that's what I'll do, and General Chase, he'll deport me, or arrest me, and the whole rigmarole will start up again.

"I get a lot of fun out of this, I do!"[1] *she says with a chuckle.*

She's been talking to herself a lot, since there's been no one else to talk to during the nine long weeks she been a prisoner.

Suddenly she hears footsteps in the hall. Someone to spring her loose? A miner's wife bringing clean stockings? "*God knows I've pulled these over my swollen feet and legs so long that they're as holey as Swiss cheese and sorely in need of a good wash."*

Could it be a newsman from the *Denver Post,* come to interview her and spread her words to the public? Almost anyone's welcome, whoever it is out there, even John D. Rockefeller himself.

She looks up, pinches color into her cheeks, fluffs her silver-white curls and says—plenty loud enough for the visitor outside her door to hear. "I wish I was God Almighty. I would throw down something some night from heaven and get rid of the whole blood-sucking bunch!"[2]

There's a stirring from the listener in the hall, a rattling of papers. She grins, and those steel-blue eyes sparkle. Her bullhorn voice that carries clear to the back of an auditorium or across a meadow full of miners and their wives rises, *"You, out there, listen to me!"*

"That was her final legacy," says Eliot Gorn, "that out of nothing but courage, passion, and commitment, she created a unique voice, a prophetic voice, and raised it in the cause of renewing America's democratic promise."[3]

She signs off on her memo, as if she's written a love letter to the laborers in the steel mills; to the railroad conductors and ironworkers; to the streetcar men, the bottle washerwomen, the children in the mills of Pennsylvania, and to her boys in the Colorado coal mines.

"I am, believe me, always yours for a Grander Civilization. Mother Jones."[4]

Glossary

Arroyo A wide ditch to channel rushing rainwater, common in the Southwest

Bituminous coal Soft coal; burns with a smoky yellow flame, used in industrial plants

Breaker boys Young boys who stooped all day, sorting the coal into specific sizes; the coal tumbled down on them in a constant torrent

Carbide Lamps Simple lamps that produce a light by the chemical reaction of calcium carbide and water; in the early twentieth century miners wore them attached to hats

CF&I Colorado Fuel and Iron Company, owned primarily by the John D. Rockefeller family

Check-weighman The person who weighed the coal each miner dug to determine what that miner would be paid; usually hired by mine operators. Miners had no recourse if the weight was inaccurate

Coke Not a beverage or a drug, this kind of coke is distilled from coal at high temperatures for more efficient heating fuel use; coke is used to extract metals from ores

Conflagration A large disastrous fire

Culm bank/Slag heap A hill near coal mines where leftovers from marketable coal are tossed; mostly slate and rock, but may have bits of usable coal

Damps Pockets of gas, such as methane and carbonic acid, that can asphyxiate miners and erupt in deadly explosions

Dead work A miner was paid by how much coal he dug in a day, but not paid for tasks necessary for digging coal, such as clearing rubble, baling water, fortifying walls with lumber, and laying track

Down the canyon A phrase used by miners. Being sent 'down the canyon' meant a union member had been fired from his job *and* prevented from getting jobs in any other mines

Falsetto A high-pitched voice

Infanticide The murder of infants

Infiltrate To sneak into and become part of a group in order to gain information

Massacre Intentional killing of people in large numbers

Martial law The law enforced by military troops in an emergency

Phalanx A troop formation so tight that enemies cannot penetrate the line

Pidgin A simplified speech used for communication by people who speak different languages

Plummeted Fell straight down or experienced a sharp decline, as in prices

Prohibition A reform movement that sought to make the sale or manufacture of alcoholic beverages illegal. When the Eighteenth Amendment to the U. S. Constitution passed, buying or selling alcohol was against the law. This was the law of the land from 1920 until 1933.

Scabs A derogatory term referring to a person who crosses a picket line and goes to work during a union strike; another word for strikebreaker

Strike To stop work for the purpose of forcing an employer to meet worker demands

Trap boys Boys who opened and closed the doors underground for the mules that pulled rail cars filled with tons of coal; a lonely job in a cold, damp cave

Tyrolean A native or inhabitant of Tyrol, a region in western Austria and northern Italy.

UMW or UMWA (United Mine Workers of America), the largest and most successful union safeguarding coal miners' interests; now called UMW, because it functions in Canada, as well as the United States

Undercutting A step in the process of extracting coal involving a three- or four-foot cut into the base of a seam of coal; this resulted in a hanging cliff of a ton of coal under which the miner worked

Timeline

1830 or 1837	Mary Harris is born in Cork, Ireland
1850s	Emigrates to Toronto, Canada; teaches school in Toronto and Monroe, Michigan
1859	Moves to Chicago to work as dressmaker
1860–1867	Moves to Memphis; marries George E. Jones and becomes involved in labor issues; gives birth to four children
1867	Husband and children die in yellow fever epidemic; moves back to Chicago to resume dressmaking
1871	Great Chicago fire destroys her dress shop
1870s–1900	Becomes active in labor struggles around the U.S., especially among coal miners in Pennsylvania; is hired by UMWA to organize miners
1901–1902	Adopts "Mother" as her working name, her persona
1902	Begins what will be years, off and on, of West Virginia organizing, strikes, violent encounters, and jailings

1903	Leads Children's Crusade of Pennsylvania millworkers to appeal to President Theodore Roosevelt on behalf of child labor conditions
1903–1904	Gets deeply involved in coal miners' strikes in northern and southern Colorado coal fields; convinces northern miners not to sign separate strike settlement agreement, which would abandon southern miners; strike ends with little benefit to miners
1904–1905	Disillusioned with the UMW, helps form Western Federation of Miners and Industrial Workers of the World
1906–1907	Raises defense funds for union leaders indicted on trumped-up murder charges; they're acquitted; gets involved with political/labor issues in Mexico
1908–1911	Travels from one location of labor upheaval to another: Pennsylvania, New York, Wisconsin, Arizona, Minnesota, and Mexico
1911–1912	Returns to West Virginia to battle military despotism during coal miner strikes
1912–1913	Convicted of charge of conspiracy to commit murder, and sentenced to 20 years in prison; freed suddenly by new governor of West Virginia
1913	Aids copper mine strikers in Montana; goes to southern Colorado as a new strike is starting
1913–1914	Imprisoned three times in Las Animas and Huerfano Counties in Colorado; incites coal miners to go out on strike in September 1913
1914	(January) Mother Jones Riot in Trinidad, Colorado; (April) Ludlow Massacre, followed by Ten Day War; travels the country telling about the strike and rallying support for miners; testifies before House Subcommittee on Mines and Mining in Washington, D.C.; asks President Wilson to intervene in Colorado and to seize mines; (December) strike ends in defeat for miners
1915	(January) Visits Rockefeller in New York to try to persuade him to go to Colorado to see the tense situation firsthand; testifies before U.S. Commission on Industrial Relations on the southern Colorado situation

1916	Aids New York and Texas streetcar workers and New York garment workers
1917–1919	Returns to West Virginia to bolster disgruntled coal miners; supports start of World War II; New York Times calls her an "apostle of violence"
1919	Leads protest against conditions in West Virginia prison; aids in steel strike; arrested several times for speaking without a permit
1920–1921	Lends support for Mexican Revolution; returns to West Virginia
1921–1923	Gives more rallying speeches around the country
1923–1924	Writes her autobiography with help from Mary Field Parton
1924–1928	In failing health, makes fewer public appearances but continues to stay involved with labor movement through correspondence; autobiography published in 1925
1928–1930	Moves in with Maryland friends Lillie May and Walter Burgess, who care for her during her last years
1930	(May) Celebrates her one hundredth birthday, at age ninety-three; (November) dies quietly at home; her body is taken to Mount Olive, Illinois, for burial with "my boys" at the Union Miners Cemetery
1936	Monument is erected in her memory at Union Miners Cemetery, Mount Olive
1984	Inducted into National Women's Hall of Fame, Seneca Falls, New York
1992	Inducted into the Labor Hall of Fame in Washington, D.C.

EVENTS DURING MOTHER JONES'S LIFETIME	
1860	Pony Express begins
1861–1865	U. S. Civil War
1861	Colorado Territory established
1865	Thirteenth Amendment to U. S. Constitution, outlawing slavery
1870	Fifteenth Amendment to U. S. Constitution, prohibiting denial of suffrage based on race, color, or previous condition of servitude
1876	Colorado becomes a state
1876	Alexander Graham Bell invents the telephone
1878	Yellow fever epidemic kills 14,000 in southern U.S.
1879	Thomas Edison invents the light bulb
1903	First baseball World Series
1907	Coal mine explosion in West Virginia kills 361 miners
1912	Titanic sinks
1913	Woodrow Wilson becomes president of the U.S.
1913	150,000 New York garment workers begin successful 3-month strike
1914	Panama Canal completed
1914	World War I starts (ends 1918)
1917	U. S. enters World War I
1919	Eighteenth Amendment to U.S. Constitution, prohibiting alcohol
1920	Nineteenth Amendment to U.S. Constitution, granting women suffrage
1927	Charles Lindbergh makes first trans-Atlantic flight
1930	Life expectancy is 61 years

Endnotes

CHAPTER ONE ~ "THE MOTHER JONES RIOT"

[1] Philip S. Foner, ed., *Mother Jones Speaks: Speeches and Writings of a Working-Class Fighter* (New York: Pathfinder, 1983), 239.

[2] Barron B. Beshoar, *Out of the Depth: The Story of John R. Lawson, A Labor Leader* (Denver: Golden Bell Press, 1942), 133.

[3] Priscilla Long, *Where the Sun Never Shines: A History of America's Bloody Coal Industry* (New York: Paragon House, 1989), 285.

[4] Zeese Papinikolas, *Buried Unsung: Louis Tikas and the Ludlow Massacre* (Lincoln: University of Nebraska Press, 1991), 172.

[5] Beshoar, *Out of the Depths*, 133.

[6] Long, *Where the Sun Never Shines*, 284.

[7] According to Mary Thomas's questionable recollection sixty years after the fact, this jailhouse fracas occurred in April 1914, immediately after the Ludlow Massacre. Most accounts place it here, in January 1914, during the Mother Jones Riot.

[8] Mary Harris Jones, *Autobiography of Mother Jones*, ed. Mary Field Parton (New York: Dover Publications, 2004), 88. Note: This edition is the unabridged republication of the original (Chicago: Charles H. Kerr and Company, 1925).

[9] George S. McGovern and Leonard Guttridge, *The Great Coalfield War* (Boston: Houghton Mifflin, 1972), 174.

Chapter Two ~ Fire Eater

[1] Foner, *Mother Jones Speaks*, 239.

[2] Ibid., 63.

[3] Beshoar, *Out of the Depths*, 32.

[4] Papanikolas, *Buried Unsung*, 166.

[5] "Conditions in the Paint Creek District, West Virginia," U.S. Senate Sub-committee on Education and Labor, Part 3, October 29, 1913, p. 2273. This statement is entered into testimony from a speech by Mary Harris (Mother) Jones on the capitol steps of Charleston, West Virginia, August 15, 1912.

Chapter Three ~ Disaster Strikes

[1] "Yellow Fever," MemphisHistory.com, accessed September 24, 2010. http://memphishistory.org/events/yellowfever/tabid/3;70/default.aspx Note: For an excellent exploration of the impact of the yellow fever epidemic in Memphis, see Molly Caldwell Crosby, *The American Plague: The Untold Story of Yellow Fever, the Epidemic That Shaped Our History* (New York: Berkeley Books, 2006).

[2] Elliott J. Gorn, *Mother Jones: The Most Dangerous Woman in America* (New York: Hill and Wang, 2001), 8.

[3] Ibid., 3.

Chapter Four ~ Tumbling Down a Chute

[1] Jones, *Autobiography of Mother Jones*, 112–113.

[2] Stephen Currie, *We Have Marched Together: The Working Children's Crusade* (Minneapolis: Lerner Publications, 1997), 53.

[3] Linda Atkinson, *The Most Dangerous Woman in America* (New York: Crown, 1978), 114–115.

[4] Gorn, *Mother Jones*, 129.

Chapter Five ~ More School, Less Hospital

[1] Foner, *Mother Jones Speaks*, 487.

[2] Atkinson, *Most Dangerous Woman*, 114.

CHAPTER SIX ~ TUG-OF-WAR – 1877-1900

[1] *Trinidad Chronicle-News*, November 22, 1913.

[2] *Trinidad Chronicle-News*, April 17, 1914.

[3] Edward M. Steel, ed., *The Correspondence of Mother Jones* (Pittsburgh: University of Pittsburgh Press, 1985), 169–170.

[4] Gorn, *Mother Jones*, 238.

[5] Papanikolas, *Buried Unsung*, 166.

CHAPTER SEVEN ~ RAT HOLES

[1] Dale Fetherling, *Mother Jones the Miners' Angel: A Portrait* (Carbondale: Southern Illinois University, 1974), 74-76.

[2] Foner, *Mother Jones Speaks*, 457

[3] Long, *Where the Sun Never Shines*, 270.

[4] Richard J. Clyne, *Coal People: Life in Southern Colorado's Company Towns 1890–1930* (Denver: Colorado Historical Society, 1999), 54.

[5] Foner, *Mother Jones Speaks*, 106.

[6] McGovern and Guttridge, *Great Coalfield War*, 277.

[7] Foner, *Mother Jones Speaks*, 253.

CHAPTER EIGHT ~ "PLUCK ME" STORES

[1] Clyne, *Coal People*, 1.

[2] Mary Harris Jones, *Autobiography of Mother Jones*, edited by Mary Field Parton. (New York: Dover Publications, 2004), 88.

[3] Ibid.

[4] Long, *Where the Sun Never Shines*, 27.

[5] Foner, *Mother Jones Speaks*, 504–505.

[6] Steel, *Correspondence of Mother Jones*, 32.

[7] Clyne, *Coal People*, 27.

[8] Susan Campbell Bartoletti, *Growing Up in Coal Country* (Boston: Houghton Mifflin, 1966), 66–67.

[9] Foner, *Mother Jones Speaks*, 74.

[10] Long, *Where the Sun Never Shines*, 50.

[11] "Faces of Black Lung," Centers for Disease Control and Prevention

and the National Institute for Occupational Safety and Health, video, 2008, accessed October 1, 2010. http://video.google.com/videoplay?docid=-8902515544143980345#.

CHAPTER NINE ~ ROARING WHIRLING OF FLAMING AIR

[1] Jones, *Autobiography of Mother Jones*, 68.

[2] Currie, *We Have Marched Together*, 20–22.

[3] Jones, *Autobiography of Mother Jones*, 55.

[4] Foner, *Mother Jones Speaks*, 239.

[5] Steel, *Correspondence of Mother Jones*, 29.

[6] Ibid., 11.

[7] Liane "Buffie" McFadyen, from speech at the dedication of Ludlow as a National Monument, June 28, 2009.

[8] Dale Featherling, *Mother Jones the Miners' Angel; a Portrait.* (Carbondale: Southern Illinois University, 1974), 109–110.

[9] Long, *Where the Sun Never Shines*, 45.

CHAPTER TEN ~ "HIT 'EM AGAIN, MOTHER JONES!"

[1] Gorn, *Mother Jones*, 3.

[2] Ibid., 235.

[3] Foner, *Mother Jones Speaks*, 85.

[4] Beshoar, *Out of the Depths*, 2.

[5] McGovern and Guttridge, *Great Coalfield War*, 171.

[6] Gorn, *Mother Jones*, 241.

[7] Foner, *Mother Jones Speaks*, 36.

CHAPTER ELEVEN ~ "SLAVERY OR STRIKE"

[1] Jones, *Autobiography of Mother Jones*, 130.

[2] McGovern and Guttridge, *Great Coalfield War*, 86.

[3] Foner, *Mother Jones Speaks*, 234.

[4] Ibid., 234.

[5] Scott Martelle, *Blood Passion: The Ludlow Massacre and Class War in the American West* (New Brunswick, NJ: Rutgers University Press,

2007), 54.

[6] Long, *Where the Sun Never Shines*, 269.

[7] Jones, *Autobiography of Mother Jones*, 140.

[8] Ibid., 234.

[9] Foner, *Mother Jones*, 237.

[10] Martelle, *Blood Passion*, 71–72.

[11] Beshoar, *Out of the Depths*, 57–59.

[12] Martelle, *Blood Passion*, 74.

[13] Foner, *Mother Jones Speaks*, 233.

CHAPTER TWELVE ~ STRIKE!

[1] Jones, *Autobiography of Mother Jones*, 155.

[2] Foner, *Mother Jones Speaks*, 512.

CHAPTER THIRTEEN ~ "EXODUS OF WOE" – SEPTEMBER, 1913

[1] Atkinson, *Most Dangerous Woman*, 188–190.

[2] McGovern and Guttridge, *Great Coalfield War*, 104–105.

[3] Gorn, *Mother Jones*, 200.

[4] McGovern and Guttridge, *Great Coalfield War*, 105.

[5] Gluck, "I Started Filling Rifles."

[6] McGovern and Guttridge, *Great Coalfield War*, 105.

[7] Judith Pinkerton Josephson, *Mother Jones: Fierce Fighter for Workers' Rights* (Minneapolis: Lerner Publications, 1997), 116

[8] Atkinson, *Most Dangerous Woman*, 187.

CHAPTER FOURTEEN ~ DUCKING GUNFIRE

[1] Beshoar, Out of the Depths, 70–74. From "Conditions in the Coal Mines of Colorado," U.S., 63rd Congress, 2nd session, House Sub-Committee on Mines and Mining, 2 vols, 1914.

[2] Beshoar, *Out of the Depths*, 74.

[3] Foner, *Mother Jones Speaks*, 378.

[4] *Trinidad Chronicle-News*, November 21, 1913 to June 22, 1914, microfilm spool.

[5] Josephine Bazanelle, exhibit notes at Ludlow Monument site. (Mrs. Bazanelle was the wife of a striking miner in Ludlow Tent Colony.)

[6] Jaclyn Gier and Laurie Mercier, *Mining Women: Gender in the Development of a Global Industry, 1670 to the Present* (New York: St. Martin's Press, 2006),184.

[7] Verlo, Eric, "Ludlow Massacre or Unhappy Incident?" Not My Tribe, April 11, 2009, http://notmytribe.com/2009/ludlow-massacre-or-unhappy-incident-87338.html.

[8] Papanikolas, *Buried Unsung*, 175.

Chapter Fifteen ~ Baseball and the Bloomer Girls

[1] McGovern and Guttridge, *Great Coalfield War*, 51–52.

[2] Papanikolas, *Buried Unsung*, 163.

[3] Clyne, *Coal People*, 60.

[4] Beshoar, *Out of the Depths*, 75.

[5] Elizabeth Jameson, from a speech at the dedication of Ludlow as a National Historic Landmark ceremony, June 28, 2009.

[6] Clyne, Coal People, 57.

[7] LeRoy R. Hafen, *Colorado and Its People: A Narrative and Topical History of the Centennial State*, Vol. I (New York: Lewis Historical Publishing Company, 1948), 486.

Chapter Sixteen ~ Scabs

[1] Steel, *Correspondence of Mother Jones*, 117.

[2] Steel, *Correspondence of Mother Jones*, 35.

[3] Atkinson, *Most Dangerous Woman*, 7.

[4] Papanikolas, *Buried Unsung*, 167.

[5] Beshoar, *Out of the Depths*, 79.

[6] McGovern and Guttridge, *Great Coalfield War*, 139.

[7] Gier and Mercier, *Mining Women*, 184.

[8] Foner, *Mother Jones Speaks*, 238.

[9] Ibid., 254. From *Vancouver Daily Province*, June 11, 1914.

[10] Jones, *Autobiography of Mother Jones*, 98.

CHAPTER SEVENTEEN ~ A DIFFERENT CHRISTMAS

[1] McGovern and Guttridge, *Great Coalfield War,* 164–165.

[2] Gorn, *Mother Jones*, 203.

[3] *Trinidad Chronicle-News*, January 12, 1914.

[4] Steel, *Correspondence of Mother Jones*, 122.

[5] Beshoar, *Out of the Depths*, 131.

CHAPTER EIGHTEEN ~ HIGH-CLASS BURGLAR

[1] *Trinidad Chronicle-News*, January 15, 1914.

[2] Beshoar, *Out of the Depths*, 132.

[3] Jones, *Autobiography of Mother Jones*, 112.

[4] Steel, *Correspondence of Mother Jones*, 125–126.

[5] Foner, *Mother Jones Speaks*, 253.

[6] Atkinson, *Most Dangerous Woman*, 201.

[7] Fetherling, *Mother Jones the Miners' Angel*, 124.

[8] Currie, *We Have Marched Together*, 39.

[9] McGovern and Guttridge, *Great Coalfield War*, 318.

[10] Ibid.

CHAPTER NINETEEN ~ "FOUR FEET OF FEATHERS"

[1] Gorn, *Mother Jones*, 119.

[2] Ibid., 161.

[3] Jones, *Autobiography of Mother Jones*, 125.

[4] Beshoar, *Out of the Depths*, 31–32.

[5] Fetherling, *Mother Jones the Miners' Angel*, 117.

[6] Priscilla Long, *Mother Jones, Woman Organizer* (Boston: Red Sun Press, 1981), 30.

[7] Ibid., 35.

[8] Josephson, *Fierce Fighter*, 125.

[9] Gorn, *Mother Jones*, 232.

[10] Ibid., 230.

[11] Foner, *Mother Jones Speaks*, 509.

[12] Gorn, *Mother Jones*, 216.

[13] Papanikolas, *Buried Unsung*, 306.

Chapter Twenty ~ Tinwillies and Fierce Warriors

[1] Long, *Where the Sun Never Shines*, 283.

[2] Papanikolas, *Buried Unsung*, 164.

[3] Gorn, *Mother Jones*, 121.

[4] Martelle, *Blood Passion*, 82.

[5] *Trinidad Chronicle-News*, January 12, 1914.

[6] Foner, *Mother Jones Speaks*, 284.

[7] Long, *Where the Sun Never Shines*, 282.

[8] Clyne, *Coal People*, 87.

[9] Gorn, *Mother Jones*, 302.

[10] Papanikolas, *Unsung Hero*, 163.

[11] Beshoar, *Out of the Depths*, 199.

[12] Josephson, *Fierce Fighter*, 125–126.

Chapter Twenty-One ~ A Great Principle

[1] McGovern and Guttridge, *Great Coalfield War*, 171.

[2] Long, *Where the Sun Never Shines*, 288.

[3] Jones, *Autobiography of Mother Jones*, 115.

[4] McGovern and Guttridge, *Great Coalfield War*, 201.

[5] Fetherling, *Mother Jones the Miners' Angel*, 125.

[6] Atkinson, *Most Dangerous Woman*, 205.

[7] Long, *Where the Sun Never Shines*, 275.

[8] Martelle, *Blood Passion*, 160.

[9] Fetherling, *Mother Jones the Miners' Angel*, 91.

Chapter Twenty-Two ~ Warlike Spirit

[1] Long, *Where the Sun Never Shines*, 278.

[2] McGovern and Guttridge, *Great Coalfield War*, 214.

[3] Ibid., 216.

[4] U.S. Department of Interior, National Park Service, National Register of Historic Places Registration Form, accessed April 28, 2010, http://www.nps.gov/nhl/Fall08Nominations/ludlow%20final%20draft.pdf, page 24. This is the 66-page application for Ludlow's designation as a National Historic Landmark. Currently http://www.nps.gov/nhl is the portal to Department of Interior information on Ludlow (accessed September 26, 2010).

[5] McGovern and Guttridge, *Great Coalfield War,* 216.

[6] Martelle, *Blood Passion,* 167. Note: Helen Korich's oral history is under her married name, Helen Krmpotich, at East Tennessee State University.

[7] Ibid.

CHAPTER TWENTY-THREE ~ LOUIS TIKAS

[1] Martelle, *Blood Passion,* 169.

[5] Martelle, *Blood Passion,* 161–162.

[6] Papanikolas, *Unsung Hero,* 171.

[7] Martelle, *Blood Passion,* 175.

[8] Ibid., 176, 244.

[9] "Eyewitness to Murder: Recounting the Ludlow Massacre," History Matters: The U.S. Survey Course on the Web, accessed April 28, 2010, http://historymatters.gmu.edu/d/5737.

[10] Papanikolas, *Unsung Hero,* 170.

CHAPTER TWENTY-FOUR ~ THE THIRTEEN

[1] Atkinson, *Most Dangerous Woman,* 207.

[2] Martelle, *Blood Passion,* 172.

[3] Las Animas County, Colorado, *Coroner's Report,* vol. 7, May 6, 1914 (microfilm spool March 31 to August 25, 1914).

[4] "Eyewitness to Murder."

[5] McGovern and Guttridge, *Great Coalfield War,* 225.

[6] Ibid., 224.

[7] Ibid., 226, 230.

[8] Papanikolas, *Buried Unsung,* 227.

Chapter Twenty-Five ~ Remember Ludlow!

[1] *Trinidad Chronicle-News*, April 21, 1914.

[2] *Rocky Mountain News*, April 22, 1914.

[3] Foner, *Mother Jones Speaks*, 246.

[4] Beshoar, *Out of the Depths*, 212.

[5] Ibid.

Chapter Twenty-Six ~ Female Power in Action

[1] McGovern and Guttridge, *Great Coalfield War*, 252.

[2] Ibid., 254.

[3] Beshoar, *Out of the Depths*, 212.

[4] Foner, *Mother Jones Speaks*, 387.

[5] Fetherling, *Mother Jones the Miners' Angel*, 133.

[6] Beshoar, *Out of the Depths*, 212.

Chapter Twenty-Seven ~ The Ten Day War

[1] Atkinson, *Most Dangerous Woman*, 207.

[2] Tomas Mariano, *Western Tales of Southern Colorado* (Trinidad, CO: Minuteman Press, 1990), 76.

[3] Beshoar, *Out of the Depths*, 193.

[4] Ibid., 192.

[5] McGovern and Guttridge, *Great Coalfield War*, 273.

[6] Jameson speech at dedication of Ludlow.

[7] Long, *Where the Sun Never Shines*, 272.

Chapter Twenty-Eight ~ President Wilson's Plan

[1] Foner, *Mother Jones Speaks*, 228.

[2] McGovern and Guttridge, *Great Coalfield War*, 267.

[3] Atkinson, *Most Dangerous Woman*, 210.

[4] Beshoar, *Out of the Depths*, 221, 240.

[5] McGovern and Guttridge, *Great Coalfield War*, 300–301.

[6] Foner, *Mother Jones Speaks*, 518.

[7] Note: According to the U.S. Census Bureau, the population of the United States in 1914 was about 99 million, as compared to today's population of about 308 million.

[8] McGovern and Guttridge, *Great Coalfield War*, 310.

[9] Jones, *Autobiography of Mother Jones*, 124.

CHAPTER TWENTY-NINE ~ MASSACRE OR NOT?

[1] Verlo, "Ludlow Massacre."

[2] McGovern and Guttridge, *Great Coalfield War*, 344.

[3] Martelle, *Blood Passion*, 160.

[4] "The Archaeology of the 1913–1914 Colorado Coal Field War Project," accessed November 4, 2010, http://www.du.edu/ludlow/cfarch.html.

[5] Verlo, "Ludlow Massacre."

[6] Mark Wolf, "Scott Martelle on His Book *Blood Passion: The Ludlow Massacre and Class War in the American West*," *Rocky Talk Live* (blog), August 23, 2007, http://blogs.rockmountainnews.com/rockytalklive/archives/2007/08/scott_martelle_on_his_book_blo.html/ (site discontinued).

[7] Verlo, "Ludlow Massacre."

[8] Wolf, "Scott Martelle on His Book."

CHAPTER THIRTY ~ ROCKEFELLER HAS A PLAN

[1] Gorn, *Mother Jones*, 218.

[2] Fetherling, *Mother Jones the Miners' Angel*, 132. In *New York Times*, May 14, 1915.

[3] Clyne, *Coal People*, 68.

[4] Beshoar, *Out of the Depths*, 250.

[5] Fetherling, *Mother Jones the Miners' Angel*, 131.

[6] McGovern and Guttridge, *Great Coalfield War*, 342.

[7] Fetherling, *Mother Jones the Miners' Angel*, 129.

Chapter Thirty-one ~ At Death's Door

[1] Steel, *Correspondence of Mother Jones*, 258. Note: The friends referenced here are Ema and Terence Powderly, of Washington, D.C.

[2] Ibid., 225, from a letter written by Terence Powderly to Mary Harris Jones, April 9, 1921.

[3] Leslie F. Orear, ed., *Mother Jones and the Union Miners Cemetery, Mount Olive, Illinois* (Chicago: Illinois Labor History Society, 2002), 81.

[4] Steel, *Correspondence of Mother Jones*, 241–242. Note: The word *gone* in this context means that the union was unsuccessful in organizing in those states.

[5] Ibid., 309.

[6] Ibid., 318.

[7] Ibid., 241.

[8] Foner, *Mother Jones Speaks*, 508.

[9] Steel, *Correspondence of Mother Jones*, 335.

[10] Atkinson, *Most Dangerous Woman*, 5.

[11] Orear, *Union Miners Cemetery*, 59–60. Originally in Lillie May Burgess, "The Last Years of Mother Jones: Personal Reminiscences," unpublished manuscript, West Virginia and Regional History Collection, West Virginia University Libraries.

Chapter Thirty-two ~ National Landmark

[1] McGovern and Guttridge, *Great Coalfield War*, 340.

[2] Gorn, *Mother Jones*, 300–301.

Chapter Thirty-three ~ Eighty Tons of Granite

[1] Foner, *Mother Jones Speaks*, 695.

[2] Fetherling, *Mother Jones the Miners' Angel*, 206–208.

[3] Foner, *Mother Jones Speaks*, 45.

CHAPTER THIRTY-FOUR ~ LEGACY

[1] Ben Fogelberg and Steve Grinstead, *Walking into Colorado's Past: 50 Front Range History Hikes* (Englewood, CO: Westcliffe Publishers, 2006), 230–231.

[2] Foner, *Mother Jones Speaks*, 501.

[3] Gorn, *Mother Jones*, 199.

[4] Ibid., 239.

[5] Ibid., 374.

[6] Ibid., 302.

[7] Ibid.

[8] "History of Mine Safety and Health Legislation," U.S. Department of Labor, Mine Safety and Health Administration, accessed October 31, 2010, http://www.msha.gov/mshainfo/mshainf2.htm/.

EPILOGUE

[1] Foner, *Mother Jones Speaks*, 494.

[2] Ibid., 199. From a speech at a meeting of striking coal miners, capitol steps, Charleston, West Virginia, August 15, 1912.

[3] Gorn, *Mother Jones*, 303.

[4] Steel, *Correspondence of Mother Jones*, 91.

Photo Credits

PAGE viii: Bain Collection, Library of Congress, LC-B2-3049-6.

PAGE 5: Denver Public Library, Western History Collection, X-60505.

PAGE 6: Denver Public Library, Western History Collection, X-60519.

PAGE 13: Library of Congress Prints and Photographs Division, LC-DIG-hec-04900.

PAGE 19: Library of Congress Prints and Photographs Division, LC-DIG-pga-00762.

PAGE 21: Library of Congress Prints & Photographs Division, LOT 12283, v. 2.

PAGE 25: Library of Congress Prints and Photographs Division, LC-D4-32069.

PAGE 26: Library of Congress Prints and Photographs Division, LC-USZ62-20508. Photographer: Lewis Wickes Hine.

PAGE 35: Denver Public Library, Western History Department, X60533.

PAGE 42: Library of Congress Prints and Photographs Division, LC-D420-2350.

PAGE 51: Library of Congress Prints and Photographs Division, LC-USZ62-77534.

PAGE 72 Denver Public Library, Western History Collection, X-60380

PAGE 75: Western History Collection, Denver Public Library X-60448.

PAGE 78: Denver Public Library, Western History Collection, X-60461

PAGE 84: Denver Public Library, Western History Collection, X-60525

PAGE 94: Denver Public Library, Western History Collection, X-60486

PAGE 97: Library of Congress Prints and Photographs Division LC-USZ62-48511

PAGE 101: Library of Congress Prints and Photographs Division rbcmil scrp4003801

PAGE 102: Library of Congress Prints and Photographs Division LC-USZC2-1053

PAGE 104: Denver Public Library, Western History Collection, Z-217

PAGE 120: Denver Public Library, Western History Collection, X-60543

PAGE 124: Used by permission, Utah State Historical Society, all rights reserved C-239

PAGE 134: Library of Congress, Library of Congress, Prints and Photographs Division, LC-Dig-15859

PAGE 138: Denver Public Library, Western History Collection, Z-214

PAGE 142: Denver Public Library, Western History Collection, X-60442

PAGE 163: Library of Congress, Digital Images Collection, LC-USZ62-50378

PAGE 167: Photograph by Fletcher L. Hill. Used by permission.

PAGE 174: Abraham Lincoln Presidential Library & Museum (ALPLM)

Bibliography

Books

Atkinson, Linda. *The Most Dangerous Woman in America*. New York: Crown, 1978.

Bartoletti, Susan Campbell. *A Coal Miner's Bride: The Diary of Anetka Kaminska*. New York: Scholastic, 2000.

Bartoletti, Susan Campbell. *Growing Up in Coal Country*. Boston: Houghton Mifflin, 1966.

Beshoar, Barron B. *Out of the Depths: The Story of John R. Lawson, A Labor Leader*. Denver: Golden Bell Press, Colorado Labor History Committee, 1942.

Clyne, Richard J. *Coal People: Life in Southern Colorado's Company Towns, 1890–1930*. Denver: Colorado Historical Society, 1999.

Currie, Stephen. *We Have Marched Together: The Working Children's Crusade*. Minneapolis: Lerner Publications, 1997.

Farrell, Mary Cronk. *Fire in the Hole!* New York: Clarion, 2004.

Fetherling, Dale. *Mother Jones the Miners' Angel: A Portrait*. Carbondale: Southern Illinois University Press, 1974.

Fogelberg, Ben, and Steve Grinstead. *Walking Into Colorado's Past: 50 Front Range History Hikes*. Englewood: Westcliffe Publishers, 2006.

Foner, Philip S., ed. *Mother Jones Speaks: Speeches and Writings of a Working-Class Fighter*. New York: Pathfinder, 1983.

Gier, Jaclyn, and Laurie Mercier. *Mining Women: Gender in the Development of a Global Industry, 1670 to the Present*. New York: St. Martin's Press, 2006.

Gorn, Elliott J. *Mother Jones: The Most Dangerous Woman in America*. New York: Hill and Wang, 2001.

Hafen, LeRoy R. *Colorado and Its People: A Narrative and Topical History of the Centennial State*. 4 vols. New York: Lewis Historical Publishing Company, 1948.

Jones, Mary Harris. *The Autobiography of Mother Jones*. Edited by Mary Field Parton. Chicago: Charles H. Kerr and Company, 1925. Reprinted and unabridged. New York: Dover Publications, 2004.

Josephson, Judith Pinkerton. *Mother Jones: Fierce Fighter for Workers' Rights*. Minneapolis: Lerner Publications, 1997.

Kraft, Betsy Harvey. *Mother Jones: One Woman's Fight for Labor*. New York: Clarion, 1995.

Long, Priscilla. *Mother Jones, Woman Organizer*. Boston: Red Sun Press, 1981.

Long, Priscilla. *Where the Sun Never Shines: A History of America's Bloody Coal Industry*. New York: Paragon House, 1989.

Mariano, Tomas. *Western Tales of Southern Colorado*. Trinidad: Minuteman Press, 1990.

Martelle, Scott. Blood Passion: *The Ludlow Massacre and Class War in the American West*. New Brunswick, NJ: Rutgers University Press, 2007.

McGovern, George S., and Leonard Guttridge. *The Great Coalfield War*. Boston: Houghton Mifflin, 1972.

Orear, Leslie F., ed. Mother Jones and the Union Miners Cemetery, Mount Olive, Illinois. Chicago: Illinois Labor History Society, 2002.

Papanikolas, Zeese. *Buried Unsung: Louis Tikas and the Ludlow Massacre*. Lincoln: University of Nebraska Press, 1991.

Parker, David L., Lee Engfer, and Robert Conrow. *Stolen Dreams: Portraits of Working Children*. New York: Dover Publications, 2004.

Steel, Edward M., ed. *The Correspondence of Mother Jones*. Pittsburgh: University of Pittsburgh Press, 1985.

Government Resources

Conditions in the Coal Mines of Colorado. Washington, DC: United States Congress House Subcommittee of the Committee on Mines and Mining, 63rd Congress, 2nd session, 1914.

Conditions in the Paint Creek District, West Virginia. Washington, DC: United States Senate, Sub-committee on Education and Labor, Part 3, October 29, 1913, p.2273. [This statement is entered into testimony from a speech by Mary Harris (Mother) Jones on the capitol steps of Charleston, West Virginia, August 15, 1912.]

Coroner's Report. Vol. 7, Las Animas County, Colorado. Microfilm spool March 31, 1913 to August 25, 1914.

West, George P. *Report on the Colorado Strike*. Washington, DC: United States Commission on Industrial Relations, 1915.

Newspapers and Web Sites

Colorado Bar Association. "Historical Background for the 2003 Mock Trial Competition." Accessed September 4, 2010. http://www.cobar.org/Index.cfm/ID/581/dpwfp/Historical-Forward-and-Bibliography.

Colorado Coal Field War Project, Denver University. "The Archaeology of the 1913¬–1914 Colorado Coal Field War Project." Accessed November 4, 2010. http://www.du.edu/ludlow/cfarch.html.

"Faces of Black Lung." Centers for Disease Control and Prevention and the National Institute for Occupational Safety and Health video, 13:00. 2008. Accessed October 1, 2010. http://www.cdc.gov/niosh/docs/video/2008-131.

History Matters: The U.S. Survey Course on the Web. "Eyewitness to Murder: Recounting the Ludlow Massacre." Accessed April 28, 2010. http://historymatters.gmu.edu/d/5737.

History Matters: The U.S. Survey Course on the Web. "I Started Filling Rifles: A Woman Strike Supporter Remembers the 1914 Ludlow Massacre," an interview with Mary Thomas O'Neil by Sherna Gluck. Accessed August 3, 2010. http://historymatters.gmu.edu/d/68.

MemphisHistory.com. "Yellow Fever." Accessed September 24, 2010. http://memphishistory.org/events/yellowfever/tabid/370/default.aspx.

Rocky Mountain News, April 22, 1914.

Rocky Talk Live; "Scott Martelle on His Book *Blood Passion: The Ludlow Massacre and Class War in the American West,*" blog entry by Mark Wolf, August 23, 2007. Accessed September 4, 2010. http://blogs.rockymountainnews.com/rockytalklive/archives/2007/08/scott_martelle_on_his_book_blo.html.

Santa Fe Trail Scenic and Historic Byway Colorado's Mountain Branch. "Ludlow Massacre—1914." Accessed May 10, 2011. http://www.santafetrailscenicandhistoricbyway.org/ludlow.html

Terwilliger, Cate. "Almost Like They Massacred Them Again: Ludlow Monument's Desecration Stuns Mining Community." *Colorado Springs Independent*, June 26, 2003. Accessed September 4, 2010.

http://www.csindy.com/colorado/almost-like-they-massacred-them-again/Content?oid=1119467

Trinidad (Colorado) Chronicle News. November 21, 1913 and June 22, 1914 (Microfilm).

United States Department of Interior, National Park Service. National Register of Historic Places Registration Form. Accessed April 28, 2010. http://www.nps.gov/nhl/Fall08Nominations/ludlow%20final%20draft.pdf.

United States Department of Labor, Bureau of Labor Statistics. "Compensation and Working Conditions: Compensation from before World War I through the Great Depression." Posted January 30, 2003. Accessed August 6, 2010. http://www.bis.gov/opub/cwc/cm20030124ar03p1.htm.

United States Department of Labor, Mine Safety and Health Administration. "History of Mine Safety and Health Legislation." Accessed October 31, 2010.

http://www.msha.gov/mshainfo/mshainf2.htm

Verlo, Eric. "Ludlow Massacre or Unhappy Incident?" Not My Tribe, April 11, 2009. Accessed September 1, 2010.

http://notmytribe.com/2009/ludlow-massacre-or-unhappy-incident-87338.html

Unpublished

Bazanelle, Josephine, exhibit notes at Ludlow Monument, June 28, 2009.

Jameson, Elizabeth, from a speech at the dedication of Ludlow as a National Historic Landmark, June 28, 2009.

McFadyen, Liane "Buffie," from a speech at the dedication of Ludlow as a National Monument, June 28, 2009.

About the Author

LOIS RUBY lives in Albuquerque, New Mexico, but her imagination and interests take her far beyond the Southwest. Her first career as a young adult librarian helped prepare her for a new career as a writer. Lois is the author of fifteen books including the historical novels *Journey to Jamestown*, *Shanghai Shadows*, *The Secret of Laurel Oaks*, and *Steal Away Home*.

Strike! Mother Jones and the Colorado Coal Field War is the result of years of research and a passion to tell the story of the feisty, cantankerous, and uncompromising 'mother' of the U.S. labor movement.

Contact Lois about school visits, library presentations, and signings through her website www.LoisRuby.com <http://www.LoisRuby.com> or by emailing Authors@FilterPressBooks.com

Acknowledgments

Thank-you to Doris and Tom Baker for having faith in a book that might otherwise have never seen print. My deep appreciation to the United Mine Workers of America, whose members have maintained the Ludlow Massacre site and annually commemorate the dramatic events of 1913-1914. And a huge thank-you to my husband, Dr. Tom Ruby, who drove me hundreds of miles to that site not once, but three times, hiding his embarrassment as I all but climbed up on the table to cheer when Mother Jones's name was mentioned. Thank-you, Tom, for patiently living with my writing obsessions for half a century and counting.

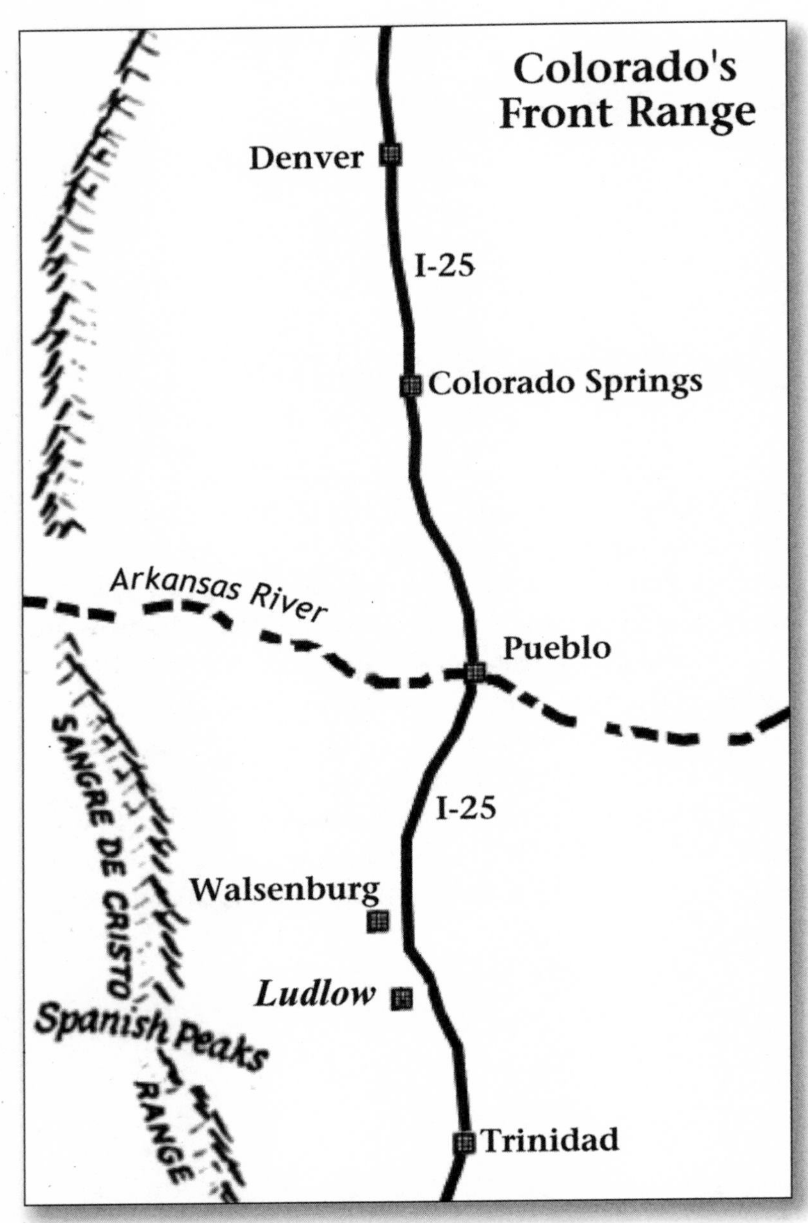

To visit the site of the events at Ludlow, drive one mile west of Exit 27 off Interstate 25 on Colorado Road 44. The site is approximately 72 miles south of Pueblo and 14 miles north of Trinidad.